BOOKS BY MICHAEL J. ARLEN

Living-Room War (1969)
Exiles (1970)
An American Verdict (1973)
Passage to Ararat (1975)
The View From Highway 1 (1976)
Thirty Seconds (1980)
The Camera Age: Essays on Television (1981)
Say Goodbye to Sam (1984)

Passage to

ARARAT

———————

Passage to

ARARAT

Michael J. Arlen

With a new introduction by
Geoffrey Wolff

Farrar, Straus and Giroux
New York

Farrar, Straus and Giroux
19 Union Square West, New York 10003

Library of Congress Control Number: 2006920041
ISBN-13: 978-0-374-53012-9
ISBN-10: 0-374-53012-2

www.fsgbooks.com

1   3   5   7   9   10   8   6   4   2

Introduction

by Geoffrey Wolff

GETTING THE WORD from Michael J. Arlen has always been a big deal; my writer friends, who don't agree on much, are pretty much unanimous on this. What a columnist wrote about the dazzling art of pitcher Lefty Grove— "[He] could throw a lamb chop past a wolf"—is true of Arlen's prose. He has it all: a tricky slider, a mystifying change-up, and a ferocious fastball blazing with anger at cruelty, cant, and hypocrisy.

Forty years ago, Arlen's coverage of television in *The New Yorker* was an ongoing cultural event. The books that collected his commentary from that period—*Living-Room War* (1969) and *The View from Highway 1* (1976)—changed the way readers viewed the medium and judged the Vietnam War. Here is a passage from "Television's War," taken from the earlier book:

> Vietnam is often referred to as "television's war," in the
> sense that this is the first war that has been brought to the
> people preponderantly by television. People indeed look at
> television. They really look at it. They look at Dick Van
> Dyke and become his friend. They look at a new Pontiac
> in a commercial and go out and buy it. They look at
> thoughtful Chet Huntley and find him thoughtful, and

at witty David Brinkley and find him witty. They look at Vietnam. They look at Vietnam, it seems, as a child kneeling in the corridor, his eye to the keyhole, looks at two grownups arguing in a locked room—the aperture of the keyhole small; the figures shadowy, mostly out of sight; the voices indistinct, isolated threats without meaning . . . Look! There is General Ky. Look! There are some planes returning safely to the *Ticonderoga*. I wonder (sometimes) what it is that the people who run television think about the war, because *they* have given us this keyhole view; we have given them the airwaves, and now, at this critical time, they have given back to us this keyhole view—and I wonder if they truly think that those isolated glimpses of elbow, face, a swirl of dress (who *is* that other person, anyway?) are all we children can really stand to see of what is going on inside that room . . .

It doesn't seem to get mentioned, for example, that we are using "anti-personnel" weapons such as the Guava and the Pineapple more than the military appears to want to admit, or that any people who drop their tortures from planes flying at five thousand feet are likely to be regarded as no less accomplices than if they had stood in person in some village square and driven little slivers of metal, at high velocity, into the flesh of other human beings. It doesn't seem to get mentioned, for example, that "anti-personnel," "delivering hardware," "pacification mission," and "nation building" are phrases, along with "better dead than Red," that only a people out of touch with the meaning of language could use with any seriousness.

And this is from the title essay of Arlen's second collection of reports and meditations on television, also directed at

the techniques—and at the political and social human conse-
quences of the techniques—of television news:

> Such might-have-beens! The networks never stood up, at
> least not for long, and, for all their billion-dollar resources,
> almost never gave their reporters honest, enterprising re-
> portorial missions—except into direct combat, which was
> mostly a false story. Each night, the great orchestration of
> the evening news went on, with its parade of surreal or su-
> perficial stories, and the vast audience traveled through
> time in its strange company. I think it is wrong or foolish
> to imagine that television news in some idealized form
> could have somehow "solved" the problem of Vietnam for
> us. But I think it is evasive and disingenuous to suppose
> that, in its unwillingness over a space of ten years to assign
> a true information-gathering function to its news opera-
> tions in Washington and Vietnam, American network
> news did much beyond contribute to the unreality, and
> thus the dysfunction, of American life.

I put these extended passages before you, readers and re-
readers of *Passage to Ararat*, first published in 1975, not
merely because I long for Arlen's unblinking sanity and
moral clarity (though it's a sure thing that we could use his
responses during these bloody seasons), but to suggest how
fiercely he might be expected to engage an act of calculated
genocide—the murder by the Turks of nearly one million
Armenians during World War I. Turkey, with feckless
brass, continues to deny the holocaust that they brought
down on their Christian neighbors in the Ottoman empire:
starved, raped, robbed, deported, death-marched, tortured,

and murdered more than half the population—men, women, and children, as it always seems necessary to specify—who lived in their territory. Reason not the reasons: wrong religion, otherness, the Turks' shame at becoming known in the condescending West at the waning of empire as "The Sick Man of Europe." And who knows, maybe just because it seemed like a good idea at the time, or because it was fun, and because they could.

Writing reflexively as a scourge against bullies—whether pricking the self-inflated, ridiculing their ascots and beach clubs, or strip-searching their cherished wisdoms—Arlen may be expected to even the odds against the underdog. He has the cutting weaponry of a Cyril Connolly or an Evelyn Waugh, with the social magnitude of a George Orwell. To describe the situation of that bombardier overflying Indochina—as akin to standing in "some village square and driv[ing] little slivers of metal, at high velocity, into the flesh of other human beings"—is to show a capacity for rage, however deliberately the writer expresses it. Imagine the fury he must have experienced studying, in obsessive detail, the Armenian genocide. From *Passage to Ararat*, here is contemporary testimony by a German eyewitness whose account Arlen studied:

> In Harpoot and Mezré the people have had to endure terrible tortures. They have had their eyebrows plucked out, their breasts cut off, their nails torn off; their torturers hew off their feet or else hammer nails into them just as they do in shoeing horses. This is all done at nighttime, and in or-

der that the people may not hear their screams and know
of their agony, soldiers are stationed round the prisons,
beating drums and blowing whistles . . .

Now, understand that regarding this horror Arlen had an
interest, a personal interest, about as personal as interests get.
His father, also Michael Arlen, was born Dikran Kouyoum-
djian, a name he changed at the insistence of the English
publisher of his first novel, *The Green Hat*, a huge success
among the London smart set of the 1920s. This change,
wrote his son in the exquisite memoir *Exiles* (1970), "I think
he was fully pleased to make; he was never much for Armenian ethnic pride, at least not when he felt it limiting."

If *Exiles* was modestly delicate, even tentative, about his
father's cultural identity, Arlen was uneasy about certain details of his father's manifestation. Remembering in that earlier book his graduation from St. Paul's School and his
father's visit there among the tow-headed station-wagoned
gentry who wore ample tweeds and worn flannels, Arlen
fretted over his father's appearance with the nearly universal
distress of a teenager: "a short dark man with a mustache, an
excessively tailored suit, a cane (he'd bought a cane, for
God's sake!)."

By the time Arlen turned to *Passage to Ararat*, he was
ready to pin down his distressful identity, and the first person he interrogated was himself. This book is an unsparing
inquisition of his deepest feelings about just who this writer
believes he is and is not, and of how, exactly, he came in this

book to judge these beliefs and feelings. He brings to his account all the formidable powers that his education, wit, experience, and style have bestowed on him, together with a lively regard for what—by way of taste, emotional expression, and easy empathy—nature and nurture have withheld.

I mean that this is as honest a narrative as I know. The timeworn modifier "painful" deserves refreshment in its application to the kind of honesty—"brutal" candor—that you'll experience when you read the story that follows. Truth-telling is, of course, an ambition rather than an achievement. If the facts in such a narrative are slippery—how many dead, under what circumstances, at the hands of which and how many murderers, with what encouragement or provocation from the State, with what cooperation or incitement from the victims—the response of the teller to these facts, however contingent in their details, can be conveyed. By an artist.

Michael J. Arlen is an artist, and his most notable art is to replicate and improvise on the astounding range of the human voice. Discussing this book recently with a fellow admirer, my friend quoted from memory a passage he'd read in *Exiles* thirty years ago. Here it is, concerning an incident from Arlen's adolescence, set in a stuffy American resort hotel at dinner with his titled Greek mother and urbane father. His parents have just been asked by a cheerful and wholesome young waitress to consider and select from the temptations, among them candied apples, offered on the relish tray. Father and mother disdain the offering, with rolling eyes and no little irony: they "complain their way through dinner. I would squirm my way, conscious of every assault delivered by them against the system, which seemed a perfectly okay system to me. (I liked relish trays, relish trays were wonderful, who would want to be so odd and alien as not to embrace a relish tray?)"

Arlen's voice—until it gathers steam and volume, going from snowball to avalanche, clearing its path inexorably—seems reassuring; it's as deliberate and formal in its deceptive proprieties as a code of chivalry, but—like a duel, whatever the contest's protocols—capable of drawing killing blood. Consider this short passage from *Exiles*: "There have been so many times when I have railed and wriggled out of being taken for my father's son, my father's second." How much is confessed, compressed into that passive construction ("being taken for") and what a choice is "second"—next in rank, dishonored duelist's advocate, junior, offspring. The passage follows unexpectedly the scene of his mother's deathbed, her son at her side, "my hand on her arm, an effort of will to make my hand a living presence, not one of those damned gestures."

Distinguishing between "damned gestures" and what he authentically felt about Armenians, their massacre, and their inevitable recapitulations of the horrors of that massacre—distinguishing between what he felt and what he believed he ought to have felt—is the grand purpose of Arlen's *Passage to Ararat*.

It is a useful and consoling convention to refer to events

and circumstances in a book in the present tense: this animates the urgent immediacy of the reader's experience as well as ameliorating the writer's mortality. I use the past tense to refer to this book's stringencies because during the course of its pages, Arlen moves from feeling one way to feeling another. In his early pages he admits that "there seemed to be something slightly dangerous or second-rate in being Armenian"; he feels repelled by "starving" Armenians and their lamentations ("hideous anguish" and "unholy screams," as described in an account). With his wife he visits Erevan, in what was then Soviet Armenia, within sight—sometimes, through breaks in air pollution—of Mt. Ararat. He reads the awful histories and testimonies from 1894 and 1915; he meets survivors. Sixty-some pages into this book: "Then, because it was what I felt, I said, 'You know, I don't think I really *like* Armenians.'"

The stimulants—stylistic, emotional, cultural, personal—of this repulsion are dauntlessly investigated in the pages that follow. But the book's deepest subject is Arlen's escape from the prison of the personal toward the open air—at the hazard of all kinds of weather—of fellow-feeling. This is a hell of a trip. Near the end, reflecting on his generous Armenian guide (who has hectored, keened, assumed kinship, and infuriated his guest), Arlen declares that "I had found out in my soul that we were both Armenian, which I knew in a certain sense was neither here nor there but in another sense was nearly everything." For this writer to use the word "soul" without irony is itself an epiphany. And what he has experienced in these pages endures, as he shows in his final chapter, back in America.

"The texture of my life is American. My kin are the Armenians. Sometimes like brothers, other times like cousins— even distant cousins. At times, I wish we were closer, but it is not always a sincere wish." You can trust him.

GEOFFREY WOLFF, author of *The Duke of Deception*, is a novelist, biographer, and essayist. His most recent book is *The Edge of Maine* (2005). He lives in Bath, Maine, and (a neat trick) teaches at the University of California, Irvine.

Passage to

ARARAT

At a particular time in my life, I set out on a voyage to discover for myself what it is to be Armenian. For although I myself am Armenian, or part Armenian, until then I knew nothing about either Armenians or Armenia. That is, almost nothing. My father had been Armenian—a child born of Armenian parents—but he had been brought up in England and educated in English schools. His citizenship had been English and, later, American. More to the point, he seemed to have virtually no connection with Armenia. At home, he never spoke the language. He rarely talked about Armenia. Professionally, he was a writer of romantic novels that were set for the most part in English society, and with hardly more than one or two exceptions he never wrote about Armenia—or Armenians. The exceptions were mainly deprecatory or amusing. One of his lines went "Now who would claim he was an Armenian if he was not?" Indeed, at the age of twenty-one he had changed his name from Dikran Kouyoumjian to Michael Arlen.

My mother (who was American and Greek) sometimes called my father Dikran in private, and this was the only way I knew as a child that he was something other than—or in addition to—English. "It's an Armenian name," she ex-

(3)

plained to me one long-ago afternoon. For a while, I thought this referred to the kind of name—a private name. I understood that some of my far-off uncles were called Kouyoumjian—an odd and difficult word for a child to scrawl on a thank-you letter. But my father, while he was well disposed toward the uncles, evidently detached himself from the name. Reluctantly, and usually with a grimace, he would tell me again how to spell it. "It's ridiculous and unpronounceable," he once said, and I had reason to agree. For the most part, my father's Armenianness was a hazy and remote matter that rarely intruded into family conversation: a youthful stage of his life that he had apparently long since passed through—had passed through successfully, as if with a school degree—and now there was clearly no point in talking further about it.

It was at an English boarding school, when I was nine, that I first realized that I was myself in any way Armenian —or, at least, half Armenian. Before the Second World War, we lived in Europe—English expatriates in the South of France. But if in those days I thought at all about identity I thought that I was English. *We* were English. We spoke English. We traveled on English passports.

At school, I was assigned to room with a cheerful, tow-headed Scottish boy, MacGregor.

"Are you French, or what?" MacGregor asked me one day.

"Of course I'm not French," I said.

"You have to be French. You live in France."

"I'm English," I said.

"You *can't* be English!" said MacGregor.

The headmaster's wife helped set us straight. We sat at her table in the school dining room—a chill and drafty chamber where ancient uniformed waitresses clattered in with trays of dry toast and sardines, or sometimes baked beans, and on Sundays with silver platters holding pieces of bread covered with gravy. The headmaster's wife was a lady of cultured interests, who was active in the local theater group, and who often discoursed to us on the larger life that she glimpsed through avid reading of the London magazines and sometimes through abrupt, disastrous excursions to audition for historical pageants in the county seat. On this occasion, she announced that she had read somewhere that my father had recently published a new book. I never had much to say to such announcements. I knew that my father "wrote books" in his office, but writing in general, and his in particular, was another subject on which very little family conversation existed or was encouraged. She had not read any of his other novels, she continued, but she was sure they were very interesting. Wasn't *The Green Hat* the famous one? She had heard many good things about it. It must be fascinating, she said, to have a father who was a well-known writer. Did I, too, speak Armenian?

This last question took me by surprise. "No, I don't speak Armenian," I said. I think I added, "I've never heard anyone speak Armenian"—which was true.

"But I know I read somewhere that your father was

Armenian," she said, with a bright smile. "I thought all Armenians spoke Armenian."

Later, in our small room, MacGregor glanced up from the comic he was reading. *"Har-meenian?"* he said. "What kind of sports do they play there?"

"I don't know," I said. "I've never been there. Probably the same sports as here."

"Not cricket," said MacGregor.

"Yes, cricket," I said. "Anyway, I'm English."

"You can't be *English,*" said MacGregor.

At midterm, my father came alone to visit me, arriving in a chauffeur-driven car and carrying a box of chocolates. For the first time in my life, I thought him strange—almost a stranger. I remember looking at him surreptitiously, sneaking glances at his face—looking for what? I don't know. I wanted him to tell me that we were really English, but I didn't know how to ask.

Months later, home on vacation, I asked my mother instead. "Are we Armenian?" I felt that it was a daring question.

"Of course not," she replied, her tone kindly but brisk. "Your father's family have Armenian blood, but he is English and so are you." She showed me his passport.

As time went by, I went to other schools. In fact, as a result of the war, we moved to America, and I became more and more American, finally, at twenty-one, becoming an American citizen. I felt generally American, or perhaps for a while Anglo-American, but, clearly, there was also something missing. Something missing or added. I became conscious of being accompanied by a kind of shadow of "being Armenian," which other people sometimes noticed, or casually commented on, but which my father had said, in effect, did not exist. And so I, too, said that it did not exist.

I remember, as an older boy at school in New Hampshire, watching terrified from a fire escape while a gang of sixteen-year-olds taunted and pushed about one of their classmates, a sallow, spidery boy called Gordon, who was supposedly Jewish. What was I so terrified of, I've later wondered—for it is not an enhancing memory. I think probably this: I had gradually become aware that to be Jewish in certain Anglo-Saxon milieus was to be "different"—that is, to be alien and unprotected—and I knew that I, too, was "different," although I was somewhat protected by the camouflage of an accepted Anglo-American manner. But I felt that it was no more than a camouflage and might disappear any day. I know that as I looked down from that fire escape at poor Gordon, I thought: There but for *them* go *we*. Who were *we*? The truth is that for most of my growing up, and for much of my life, I didn't try very hard to find out. There seemed to be something slightly dangerous or second-rate in being Armenian; otherwise, my father would not have been so determined to move beyond it. And so I took the hint and followed him. Armenians were somebody else.

I remember also, years ago, in New York, around the time of an expected visit from my Uncle Krikor, who lived in Argentina, my father angrily brandishing some recent communication from Buenos Aires—probably a change in plans. "Why can't these Armenians ever do things simply?" he said. And "Now, isn't this just like an Armenian!" Evidently, Uncle Krikor was "just like an Armenian"; my father was something different. And, in fact, when Krikor finally arrived (a short, wiry man, with a definite nose and a face tanned by the Argentine sun) I felt him to be different from my father—darker, somehow more "Eastern"—although actually the two men were of the same size and build, had similar features (except for the Argentine suntan), and spoke impeccable English. At one point, Krikor addressed a few words to me in Armenian, which I naturally couldn't reply to. "Why, you haven't taught the boy any Armenian!" said Krikor, in genial reproof. We were having dinner in Krikor's hotel.

My father in those days had a carefully trimmed mustache and wore a flower in his jacket. "Well, it's an impossible language," he said, scowling.

Krikor smiled good-naturedly. "Ah, Dikran," he said. He was the elder brother.

In all my life, I never heard my father speak a single word of Armenian, unless one counts the occasional times we went to an Armenian restaurant and he would read, with a certain offhand professionalism, from the exotic menu, with its kebabs and dolmas, which, I later found out, were mainly Turkish. On the whole, I met few Armenians in his company, and most of these I thought of as being associated with a particular Armenian restaurant in New York, which we went to *en famille* perhaps once or twice a year. It was called the Golden Horn and was a small place in the West Fifties. Its proprietor was a large, warm-hearted man—Aram Salisian, a former wrestler, as wide as he was tall, with immense, gnarled hands and a square, rough-hewn, kind face, which invariably seemed to be smiling. When we entered, he always embraced my father; I think he was just about the only man I ever saw do so. He bowed to the rest of us. He told me that someday he would teach me how to wrestle.

I liked the Golden Horn, because it was a nice place and because as a family we were generally happy there. I also had a special, secret feeling about it—and still have to this day, although the restaurant itself has disappeared—for it was the only region or territory in which I can recall my father's being at case with his Armenian identity, even halfway accepting it. "So-and-So was here the other day," I can remember Salisian saying, stopping by our table, rattling off an Armenian name.

"Is that so?" I can hear my father's voice reply. "Well, how is he? Say hello to him from me."

Say hello to him from me. Not what one might describe as reckless bonhomie, but in those rare and periodic moments I believe he showed more affection for his Armenian background—our Armenian background—than most other times that I can remember. Now and then, other guests in the restaurant, or at the bar, would come over to chat for a few minutes. Talk of families, of sons and daughters in school. George, the bartender, I remember, had a son studying with Rudolf Serkin at the Curtis Institute of Music, who later became the pianist Eugene Istomin.

It was a strange and friendly time—strange because the men and women there for the most part looked to me so different, as if they were from another country, and yet for a moment we were part of them, their group, whatever *they* might be. I had a sense of "Armenia" as a fragile network of restaurants inhabited by people who seemed to live elsewhere—in somebody else's country. All that seemed real to me was the affection, the mysterious bond. On the walls of the restaurant, I remember, there were photographs of various Armenians who had "made good." One of them was a picture of my father with William Saroyan, the Armenian-American writer from California, whose plays had been appearing on Broadway and winning prizes. In the photograph, the two men were seated at a table with drinks in front of them, smoking cigarettes, staring rather glassily into the flashbulb—the usual night-club snapshot. It seemed to me a romantic and heroic moment: my father together with Mr. Saroyan. My eyes always turned to it—that glimpse of an Armenian comradeship.

But then after dinner we all walked out of the Golden Horn, saying goodbye to Mr. Salisian, leaving Aram Salisian and his world behind—and were back in our own world. On a few occasions, perhaps encouraged by our moments at the restaurant, I later questioned my father about Armenia, but I tried this rarely, because he so visibly wished not to be connected with the subject—in fact, brushed off such simple questions as I might have put—and because, indeed, I had no strong wish to be connected with it myself. Once, I remember, I asked him to come to the phone to take a call from a Mr. Hagopian, an Armenian professor who wished to discuss a literary project. "Tell him I'm out," my father said coldly. Afterward, I asked him why, for Hagopian and he had clearly never met. "He'll only want to talk about Armenian problems," my father said. "He'll go on for hours. They end up boring you to death." Later, more casually, he said, "They're a sweet people, but you can't let them get too close."

For the most part, I was content to leave things as they were. I was only slightly curious about my Armenian background—or so I thought, although, if I had understood how to acknowledge such matters, I might have known that I was haunted by it. Mostly, I was afraid of it. (What *were* "Armenian problems"? I supposed they must have to do with "Turkish massacres" and "starving Armenians," and such—distant and repellent events that I had vaguely heard about and that obviously had little or nothing to do with us.) What was I afraid of? It's difficult to remember now. Probably of being exposed in some way, or pulled down by the connection: that association of "difference," one's own "difference," with something deeply pejorative, with sin. I can't say that I felt sinful in any explicit sense, but I felt somehow marked—even to the extent, for much of my life, of considering myself unnaturally dark, so that a few years ago I was astonished to hear a skin doctor describe my skin as "light." And in the end (as perhaps in the beginning) I came to hate my father for my fear. It was not the only emotion I felt toward him, for I loved him, too; though he was seldom an emotionally expressive man, I knew, he was kind to me. He was my father. But also I was afraid of him. Something always lay between us—something unspoken and (it seemed) unreachable. We were strangers.

WHEN my father died, nineteen years ago, I felt we were no closer. Even as on his deathbed he talked with me amiably and we held each other's hands. Even as, later, I wrote about him—for I myself had become a writer, although not a novelist, and tried to make a kind of contact with him, and with my mother, by writing about their life together and his career. As I remember, his funeral service was held in a Greek Orthodox church (my mother's church), rather than in an Armenian church. "All his life, he wanted to be free of the Armenians," my mother said. I missed him, although it was a relief to me in some ways that he was gone. Absent. In truth, I dreamed about him often, usually in the same scenario, or in dreams with the same feel to them: a feeling of distance between us. Sometimes he called to me and I couldn't hear what he was saying. Sometimes he merely stood apart—a solitary and somehow disapproving figure. We were still strangers.

BY THE TIME I had turned forty, my mother was dead, too. My own identity as an American seemed to me fairly definite—at least on the surface. I had an American wife and American children—a satisfactory American career and life. Then, one day, out of the blue, I was asked by an Armenian group in New York to come down and give a talk about writing. I was surprised and flattered by the invitation—for my lecture services were not in great demand—and said yes.

I can remember the evening vividly. The talk was given in an auditorium of the Armenian Cathedral, on Second Avenue—a place I had never before visited. The audience sat before me on little chairs—middle-aged Armenian men and women, for the most part, the men generally stocky, the women wearing old fashioned flowered dresses. What I said was undistinguished, but all of a sudden I myself felt greatly moved. I remember standing at the lectern gazing into the rows of clearly Armenian faces—more Armenians than I had ever before seen together—and experiencing an extraordinary pull. My eyes told me that these people were different from me, but I knew that they were not so different. I didn't know what else I knew.

Afterward, an old gentleman with thick white hair came up to me. "An interesting talk," he said. "Although you didn't mention any Armenian writers. It's too bad we never saw your father here."

"I don't think he thought of himself as Armenian," I said. And as soon as I had said it I realized that it was untrue.

"Of course he was Armenian," said the old man. "You are Armenian. It is not such a strange thing to be Armenian. Come, have some coffee."

I think I thought something like, You can go forward here, or stay where you are. And so I went with him and had some coffee.

Such small beginnings. That evening, for the first time, I met Armenians on my own. Armenian women who laughed and asked too many questions. Thick-chested men who seemed always to have their arms around each other. Too many cups of coffee and small, sweet cakes. I was *there* —wherever *there* was. It was an uncertain beachhead, for I kept fighting off the desire to bolt. Never let them get too close! But I also knew that a corner of some missing piece had briefly become visible.

As I finally made my way toward the door, a voice called out, "You will come back!" I couldn't tell whether it was a statement or a question.

"I will," I said.

The journey had begun.

My wife said, "Did you know that Mt. Ararat was in Armenia?" She had been reading one of my new Armenian books.

I said I knew.

"Do you suppose Noah was an Armenian?"

I said I didn't think it worked that way.

Later, she said, "Tell me about the kings of Nairi."

"I don't know about them," I said.

"It says here they were your ancestors. It says, 'Many years ago, the land of Armenia was ruled over by the kings of Nairi.'"

IT IS POSSIBLE to learn nearly anything from books, except, perhaps, about the kings of Nairi. Kings, indeed! Such roughnecks as inhabited the world then! We are talking of three thousand years ago—maybe more—when the fierce and martial Assyrians clanked about Asia Minor. Five thousand years ago, when civilized life was well under way in Egypt, Babylon, and Sumer, it had also begun to appear— or, at least, leave records of itself—in certain valleys of the vast mountain plateau that stretches from the Russian

Caucasus southward between the Black and Caspian Seas and into what is now eastern Turkey. Even then, this was a land of farms and vineyards and large mineral deposits: a beautiful, remote terrain of fertile valleys and high mountain peaks, all of it, even the flat parts, elevated—much like the American West—with the average height around six thousand feet above sea level. For thousands of years, primitive peoples had lived in the valleys below the great mountains. There they had begun to tend wild vines—the vines that most likely seeded the vines of Babylon and Egypt. They had mined for tin and copper, producing bronze for the Bronze Age and metalwork for Ur of the Chaldees. They had made pottery and evolved striking geometric pottery designs, which showed up as far away as ancient Palestine and Syria. These people were a multitude of tribes, whose stock was mainly Hurrian and Hittite. Many tribes and many kings: the kings of Nairi. In fact, "Nairi" is a word that comes to us from Assyrian records, and it does not mean very much any more. It is only a word, with perhaps rather a sweet sound to it. "Twenty-three kings of the land of Nairi ordered their chariots and warriors to assemble and rose against me for war and battle," wrote a scribe of the Assyrian King Tiglath-pileser I, himself a redoubtable roughneck.

But eventually out of Nairi came the kingdom of Urartu. Now, there is a word without any sweet sound to it. Urartu . . . Ararat. Mt. Ararat, of the Genesis ark story. Later— around 600 B.C.—the Book of Jeremiah speaks of the kingdom of Ararat, as the prophet inveighs against wicked Babylon: "Set ye up a standard in the land, blow the trumpet among the nations against her, call together against her the kingdoms of Ararat, Minni, and Ashchenaz." The Urartians built towns and fortresses. They dug irrigation ditches and constructed large aqueducts. They traded with the Mediterranean communities; not only that, they bestrode one of the great natural trade routes of the world—through the mountain passes of what came to be called the Armenian plateau. The Urartians produced pottery and war chariots and armor. They borrowed cuneiform from the Assyrians, but they evolved their own speech, a descendant of the Hurrian language, which itself was unlike anything else: one of those odd languages that developed (in the remoteness of the mountains) independently of the main language systems.

The growth of Urartu threatened the Assyrians, and so the Assyrians made war on the kingdom—a difficult and essentially unrewarding occupation for the Assyrians, who year after year were compelled to march their army northward great distances into the inhospitable mountains. There is a pair of huge bronze gates now in the British Museum—carted off from an Assyrian city by some enterprising archaeologist—which depict the campaigns of King Shalmaneser III against Aramu, King of Urartu. Since this was Shalmaneser's record of the event, the Assyrians are shown to be ahead, at least to the extent of pictographs displaying burning fortresses and Urartians impaled on stakes. For the most part, the Assyrians and the Urartians fought each other, off and on, for nearly three hundred years—until both states were weakened to the point of extinction. The Assyrians probably went down first, being toppled (shortly before Jeremiah's invocation) by the Medes, and by the "Ashchenaz," who were a wave of one of the first big nomad invasions—that of the vast Asiatic tribe known to later Westerners as the Scythians, and to the Chinese as the Sai-Wang. A few years later, the kingdom of Urartu—itself beset by Medes and Scythians—started to fall apart, too, disintegrating into separate tribes, and soon ceased to exist as a nation.

Some of the tribes that had been part of Urartu remained, and in this war-torn area two new groups also made their presence felt. The smaller of these was the Armen, or Armeni, which, according to Herodotus, had migrated to the area by way of Thrace and Phrygia. The larger, and more advanced, tribe was the Hayasa, which had once been part of an ancient Hittite federation in Asia Minor. This, then, was the point at which the Armenians appeared in history—from a mingling of the Hayasa, the Armen, and the remains of the tribes of Urartu. In fact, traditionally—in their own language—the Armenians refer to themselves as Hai and to their country as Hayastan. According to ancient Armenian legend, Haik, a descendant of Japheth (one of Noah's three sons), rebelled against the Assyrian tyrant Belus some time after the destruction of the Tower of Babel and fled with his family "north to the land of Ararat." Belus went after him, "gathering a great army," and a mighty battle was fought. Haik killed Belus with a lucky arrow, and where Belus died Haik built a village, which he "caused to be named after himself." So much for legends.

The first appearance of the name Armenia is probably in an inscription set up about 520 B.C. by Darius the Great, of Achaemenid Persia, who, on a rock face about five hundred feet above the ancient road from Ecbatana to Babylon, let the world know some of the difficulties he had run into after seizing the Persian throne:

> Says Darius the King: While I was at Babylon, these nations revolted against me; namely, Persia, Susa, Media, Assyria, Arminaiya, Parthia, Margiana, Sattagidia, and Sacia.
>
> Says Darius the King: Then Dadarses by name, an Arminaiyan, one of my servants, him I sent to Arminaiya.
>
> I said unto him: Greetings to thee. If a rebel state should not obey me, smite it. Then Dadarses marched. When he reached Arminaiya, the rebels came before him, arraying their battle. Zuzza by name, a village of Arminaiya, there they engaged. The God Ahuramazda brought help to me. My forces entirely defeated the rebel army.

There is a pictograph accompanying the cuneiform: Darius, the stern teacher, stands beside his throne; the nine rebel leaders are ranged before him with ropes around their necks. Further on in the text, there is a reference to "Aracus the Arminaiyan," who is mentioned as "usurper" of no less a place than Babylon itself. "He threw Babylon into revolt," says the Great King crossly, adding, "For which he was punished." One can imagine. Here, then, were the Armenians. Mountain people. Pupils before a stern teacher. They had fought off the Assyrians, and survived the Scythians and Medes. The Persians demanded ten thousand horses a year as tribute. Cavalry was to be the weapon of the future.

I wondered what to make of these my forebears, for it was hard not to have some kind of thought about them, usually self-serving. Were they noble or ignoble? Winners or losers? I thought, What kind of crazy notion was that: Were the kings of Nairi winners or losers? It was all so far away and out of focus. My books showed hazy photographs of excavated jars and helmets from Urartu—immense earthen jars and quaint, pointy helmets. Nairi was a word, Hayasa but a shadow. The Great King Darius (who employed his own artist) came through, somehow, more clearly: an unusually large man for his time, nearly six feet tall, with thick arms and a fiercely staring eye. But it was difficult to glimpse the Armenians: Dadarses, Aracus, and all the rest. Had they always been part of someone else's story? They seemed to swim beneath the surface, far away in eddies of time.

One afternoon, I went to have tea with the white-haired old gentleman I had met at the church. It was in his apartment, on Thirty-third Street near First Avenue—not a fashionable address at first glance. One of those silent streets, with unkempt children fighting noiselessly on the sidewalk, and the dun-colored buildings waiting patiently to be torn down. Fortunately, it was not tea but brandy. We sat in the dark sitting room and discussed the condition of the city, the matter of children, and Armenian affairs. It was a soft time of day. The old gentleman spoke about Armenian music— not the fancy kind that they played in the church but what they played in "the old country." Had I ever heard the sound of the *doudek*? It was a beautiful sound, he said. He got up and went into the next room and came back with a small case. It contained a kind of flute, or reed. "It is best when two people play," he said. "Two *doudeks*. One of them holds a single note. The other plays the song. The song always gets the applause. But to hold the single note is very hard. There is a technique for it."

We sipped at the dark brandy. There were Oriental rugs on the floor. Tinted photographs of red-lipped children on the mantelpiece. A door opened quietly (a door from the outside? from a back room?), and another man entered. He was a cousin, a frail, angular man in his late sixties. He sat beside me on the faded plum-colored couch. The sunlight grew dim outside the windows. We talked some more about music, and about my father.

"Did he enjoy Armenian music?" asked the old gentleman.

"He never listened much to music," I said.

The cousin placed a hand on my arm in a feathery grip and began to talk in an intense, low voice about his family's experiences with the Turks. He described the killing of his father and his elder brother. He described the flight of his mother and his two sisters, one of whom was captured and never heard from again. "I can imagine what happened to her," he said. "The Turks were *fiends*. They knew only how to kill. We Armenians had done nothing to them. Nothing! We were simple, God-fearing people who asked only to be left to our ways. The Turks brutalized us and raped our women." He began to weep.

The old gentleman nodded soberly from across the room. He had the *doudek* on his lap. Everything inside the room was still, and the air felt thick. There were little boxes on every table, every surface. Through the open window came the sound of distant traffic. Buses. A taxi horn. The man on the couch began to speak again, this time more softly—in a kind of croon—about his boyhood, long ago. A village somewhere, the name of it unintelligible. A Turkish village? An Armenian village? He talked of running, fleeing, as a boy, across the desert. Of hiding in a cave for days. There were dead bodies in the cave. A camel driver befriended him and hid him for three weeks—or months. The story was true, I knew—a true and moving story, and one so far beyond my own experience. But I found I wished his arm away from mine, wished away his frail hand, his tears. "My father had committed no crime—can you believe it? He had done nothing wrong." I could believe it. But I wished to be away, and out in the busy street.

Later, I thought, This cannot be Armenia, this cannot be what it is. Tears. Stories of evil times. Dark interiors and the croon of old men. "My father had committed no crime." But he was killed, wasn't he, and his brothers were killed, and his sisters were destroyed, and this old man—this boy—had been made to run and hide and to become small in his fear. What kind of son was that? What kind of father?

I SOMETIMES wondered how I could learn anything about Armenians, or my father—or, indeed, myself if I could not sit still with them.

Meanwhile, my wife annoyed me by making lists of "famous Armenians": Rouben Mamoulian, the movie director; Aram Khatchaturian, the composer; Garo Yepremian, the football player; Lucine Amara, the opera singer. Did I know that the television actor Mike Connors was an Armenian (né Ohanian)? Did I know that Arlene Francis (née Kazanjian) was an Armenian? Kirk Kerkorian? Charles

Aznavour (Aznourian)? Did I know that the mayor of Waukegan was named Sabonjian?

"Stop it," I said. I knew she was trying to be helpful, but it irritated me. It was like making a list of "famous graduates" of a small, out-of-the-way college. Also, it was such an *Armenian* thing to do. I was in an irritable frame of mind. This was partly because it shamed me that I had been so put off by the two old cousins—particularly by the cousin who spoke about the Turks. The sturdy old fellow with the *doudek* I had liked and felt at ease with, but the one who lamented the destruction of his family by the Turks had put a desire for flight in my bones. I knew that it was wrong of me. I knew that he, of all people, required my sympathy. But I had found it almost physically impossible to keep my arm under his hand, and myself seated beside him listening to his voice.

What had been so hard about it? At first, I thought that I had been too repelled by his tale of misery—that the details of his tragedy, as of a friend's car accident or operation, had been too rich to stomach. But as soon as I thought this I knew that it was not so. I had never been squeamish about such things, and certainly not as a result of an old man's lamentations. I realized that, instead, I was still possessed by a kind of fear. For later, walking hurriedly away from that apartment on Thirty-third Street, I had said to myself, "I know that somewhere there exists a different type of Armenian, a prosperous, vigorous, robust type of Armenian, who does not live in dark rooms and weep about the past." I had even formed the phrase "prosperous, vigorous, robust" in my mind. And afterward, when I remembered the phrase, it embarrassed me, for the feelings I seemed to express within my head were so unaccepting that I doubted whether I could ever get close to Armenians. The old cousin's words continued to stick in my mind. "My father had committed no crime . . . had done nothing wrong," he had said, and he had added, "Yet the Turks destroyed us!" As I thought about it, there seemed to be something terrible buried in that admission, although whether the negative electrical charge I felt lay in the statement or in me I couldn't tell. Only that I hated it.

Around this time, I went to a different kind of Armenian event: a concert at the Armenian Cathedral—a recital at which perhaps a half-dozen Armenian musicians performed on the piano and the violin and the cello. The musicians all seemed serious and quite youthful, and the music was good. The audience was very dressy, and I was immediately conscious of being in the presence of many prosperous and vigorous (and doubtless robust) Armenians. Indeed, some of them barely seemed Armenian—except, of course, that they were unmistakably Armenian. During the intermission, I had a drink with two brothers, both in their forties, who apparently owned a large amount of property somewhere in New Jersey and were about to erect a "total-living complex" for thousands of families. Both men had wonderful mustaches and thick, heavy faces, and unlikely, flouncy-frilly blue shirts. They spoke in a kind of duet about property values and interest rates—serious men with booming laughs, if such a thing is possible. "Were these the kings of Nairi?" I asked myself.

After the concert, a number of us went to the apartment of another man, called Bud—also Armenian. It was a fine apartment uptown in the East Seventies, with a view of Central Park. The rooms were carefully strewn with a variety of Chinese objects—vases, screens, and such. There were several drawings by Rodin and Braque and others hanging in the foyer, which had an imitation-marble floor. We sat in a row on a long leather sofa, or else stood by the large windows and looked down upon the lamplit park. Our host's wife, a handsome Armenian woman wearing mandarin pajamas, brought around liqueurs.

"How does your name happen to be Bud?" I asked the host, for I was interested in the provenance of names.

"Actually, my real name is Yeprad, which means Euphrates," he said, "but everyone calls me Bud."

We all trooped in to see the new glass table in the dining room, which had been mounted on a piece of driftwood brought back from the Bahamas.

"How is business?" I asked Bud, for it certainly seemed to be good.

"It's very good," he said. "I deal mainly in copper, and, as you know, the price of copper is up."

We shuffled along quietly on thick carpets. A large hanging carpet with a lion design had been recently brought back from Ethiopia. Several of the guests were drinking Japanese beer.

"Would you like to see a painting I have of Mt. Ararat?" asked Bud.

I said I would.

We went into a small room off the kitchen—a maid's room that had been converted into a utility room but seemed to be rarely used. A pile of women's dresses was on a narrow bed. A sewing machine stood open on a table. On the far wall, between a watercolor of some sailboats and a child's drawing of a horse, there hung an oil painting of Mt. Ararat. It was executed, on the whole, in a modernist fashion: the mountain was a deep red, the sky was a shade of yellow; in fact, it looked rather Polynesian. We stood together admiring the painting.

"The truth is I am not very active in Armenian matters," said Bud. "That is, I am not as active as I should be."

I said, "I saw in the concert program that you're on numerous Armenian boards. Also, you were at the concert."

"Yes, I know," he said. "But I am not involved the way my parents were."

It was a thoughtful moment. I did not know what else to say.

"But look here," said Bud, brightening. "I have some Armenian books." He bent down beside a small bookcase in a corner containing a variety of books, many of which were paperback or Modern Library editions and looked as if they might have been bought at college. He held up three larger volumes, two of which I recognized, for I had recently purchased them myself: a standard Armenian history text, and an account of the Turkish massacres entitled *Armenia: The Case for a Forgotten Genocide;* the third was a travel book.

"Have you read this one?" I asked, pointing to the book about the massacres. I had opened it a few days earlier and, alternately repelled and fascinated by the photographs, had soon put it down.

Bud examined the outside of the book cautiously. "No, I've read enough about the Turks," he said. "I'm not interested any more in that business with the Turks."

One of the New Jersey real-estate brothers came into the room and caught sight of the book we were examining—or, rather, not examining. "What's this?" he said sternly, but with the same booming effect. "What do you read this for? Haven't you read enough of such things?" He seemed to be laughing and scowling at the same time.

"Yes, it's all ancient history," said Bud.

"We're Americans," said the man from New Jersey. "I was in the war."

"Aram was in Korea," Bud told me. "Did you know there were Turks on our side in Korea?"

"I have no quarrel with the Turks," said the New Jersey American called Aram. "The Turks are my brothers. I embrace the Turks!" He looked at me. "Are not all men my brothers?"

"Yes, they are," I said.

He put his arm around my shoulder. "I tell you, there is no point in raking over the past."

Later, back in the living room, I asked Bud where his parents had come from.

"Fresno, California," he said. "The San Joaquin Valley. There were many Armenians there, did you know? They came from the old country." He sighed. "It's beautiful in that valley. But I have not been back there in a long time. Many years."

"Where in the old country?" I asked.

Bud looked vague, almost amused. "Oh, it was one of those small villages in the mountains," he said.

Just then, his wife, the handsome woman in the Chinese pajamas, paused on her way through the room. She glanced at her husband with a small smile—a passing look that seemed to come from somewhere else—and for a second even her chinoiserie appeared to vanish or recede. "But, Yep," she said (it must have been short for Yeprad), "you know it was Mirash, about twenty miles from Bitlis."

"That's it," said Bud briskly. "Near Bitlis. In the old country." He got to his feet—a short, energetic man in his early fifties, with only slightly graying hair and a fine sun-tan. He grinned. He was clearly a hospitable man. "Come on, let's feed the tropical fish," he said.

I knew I should begin to read some of the "difficult" books about the Armenians—namely, the post–First World War literature on the massacres—but I found it hard to do so. It wasn't a *simple* reaction—that of not wanting to read about dreadful things, or not wanting to read about Armenians' being mistreated. At least, I told myself it wasn't that, for I felt that by then I had surely read of enough atrocities (as had most citizens of this century), enough "case histories" of pain administered and people broken—in this fashion or in that fashion, in this country or in that country—so that there could be little reason now for me suddenly to be unable to confront what the Turks had once done to the Armenians. Still, there was something about these books—buried within these stories—that bothered me inside where I had not been bothered before: something more complicated than moral nausea, more troubling than a voyeuristic shudder.

Now and then, in the evening, my wife would peer into one of my Armenian books and call out to me across the room, "My God! You won't believe how awful it was!" Then she would show me, or leave for me to read, an account of one or another dreadful happening. I remember one such passage in particular. It was an account of an Armenian priest and two Armenian schoolteachers who had been seized in their village by the Turks in 1915. The Turkish gendarmes had handed the Armenians over to a Turkish mob. The priest had been tied to a chair, and then the hair on his head and the hair of his beard had been pulled out. Then his ears had been sliced off. Then his nose. Then his eyes had been gouged out. Nails had been driven into the schoolteachers' hands and feet, as on a crucifix, and then into their heads. The account described the "hideous anguish" and "unholy screams" of the victims. As I read, I could feel my stomach churn at the physical aspect of the atrocities. But I felt something else churning inside me as well. For there seemed to be a voice behind that terrible tale which I could abide even less than the event described. Was it the voice of "hideous anguish" and "unholy screams"? Was it a more general and pervasive voice—a voice that seemed to run as an undercurrent through much of the writing about these massacres? It was hard to tell, but it made me want to weep and also to throw the book aside, away.

I remember that my wife asked me afterward, "Wasn't it terrible, what they did?"

And I felt so angry that I could hardly speak.

She saw my mood and quickly said, "Oh, I'm so sorry. Of course, they're your people."

But inside me I knew I was not angry then at the Turks—not mainly so—or, certainly, at her. I was angry at something else. But at what? It was a mystery.

AND SO I continued to read about the Armenian past —the faraway, historical past.

For example, Xenophon's *Anabasis*, which I had read thirty years before in school without noticing that much of the retreat of the Ten Thousand took place through the Armenian high country.

"They formed up together about midday and marched through Armenia [wrote Xenophon], all plain and little smooth hills. . . . This district was called Southern Armenia. The Lieutenant Governor was named Tiribazos [an Armenian, who was the King of Persia's friend] and it was his right to mount the king on horseback when he was pres-ent. . . .

"A north wind blew in their faces, parching everything and freezing the men. . . . The snow was one fathom deep, so that many animals and slaves were lost, and soldiers too, numbering about thirty. . . .

"Xenophon . . . begged them with prayer and entreaties not to fall behind . . . but they asked him to cut their throats, march they could not. . . . It was dark now and the enemy were following in confusion and quarreling over what they had. Then the rear guard [of the Hellenes] shouted as loudly as they might and banged spears against their shields."

After dodging Tiribazos and his men, the Greeks finally

descended into a warmer valley, filled with friendly Armenian villages.

"The people never let them go without offering them a feast. Everywhere on the same table there were piles of lamb, kid, pork, veal, fowl, with all manner of cakes, both wheaten and barley. . . . They found Cheirisophos and his men in their quarters, garlanded with crowns of straw and served by Armenian boys in their native costume. [Cheirisophos and Xenophon] together asked the headman, through the interpreter, who spoke Persian, which country this was. He said, The land of Armenia. They asked him for whom he was breeding the colts. He replied, They are tribute for the king. The neighboring country, he said, was the land of the Chalybeans, and pointed where the road lay."

There was something very moving in that ancient and human narrative, with its account of the dreadful march through the mountains. Tough Greek veterans, in their desert sandals, begging their commander to slit their throats in the snow! And on the rocks behind them and above them the Armenians following, a bit like Indians. Then, down in the valley, the Greeks and the Armenians had briefly come together. Sea people, inheritors of Crete, exchanging wary toasts with mountain people, inheritors of Urartu. "Cheirisophos and his men . . . garlanded with crowns of straw." Such brutal, fairy-tale times!

It seemed to me wonderful that the Armenians, *we* Armenians, should have such an ancient and textured history. Not always a glorious and victorious one, mind you. That was too much to expect of a small nation placed by God and geography on the outskirts of the world's great central empires. But clearly the Armenians had not been entirely *ignored* by large events or important empires. First, the Persians, with their ponderous palaces and their almighty god, Ahura Mazda. Compared to other nations then, Armenia was a territory of substantial size. Not only that—it was a strategic terrain, for the Armenian plateau took the shape of a kind of citadel; topographically, Armenia looked down upon the great and busy nations of the lowlands. The Persians left a local man in charge of this northern province—usually a powerful Armenian chief or landowner, whom they called satrap—and, for the most part, kept their distance, except for putting down an occasional rebellion or engaging in a religious persecution or two. And except for the horses.

In the time of Xerxes, as many as twenty-five thousand horses were sent down from Armenia to Persia every year, and in later periods the number doubled and redoubled. Twenty-five thousand horses—a considerable herd. The Armenian plateau, it turned out (in yet another parallel with the American West), was an unusually fine place to raise good horses, for the short, stubby, seemingly dry grasses were immensely rich in protein, and the high-altitude air produced a type of animal possessing exceptional speed and stamina—ideal for cavalry. Imagine a "drive" of twenty-five thousand yearlings from Armenia five hundred miles to Ecbatana!

These early Persians had such great dreams of a coherent empire. They dreamed of cavalry, the unbeatable war machine, before anyone had invented stirrups. They dreamed of a trade-and-communications network before anyone had much to trade or communicate, and so built roads westward across Asia Minor and north into Armenia. Old Darius himself always kept an eye to the north, and toward the end of his long reign—he was then an aging Persian autocrat tinkering with erratic notions of religious freedom as well as with early concepts of highway design—dispatched a military expedition into Armenia, through Armenia, through the Caucasus, and out into the Eurasian steppe, where, finding nothing, it eventually turned back. What were they looking for, these Persians standing around in the middle of the deserted Ukraine at the start of the fifth century B.C.? Darius never said.

The Persians had noticed Armenia because of its strategic position as a defense against the Scythians and because of its horses. The Greeks soon noticed it for the same reasons, and because of trade, since a natural passageway existed through the valleys and icy mountains of Armenia which connected the Eastern world with the Mediterranean and Greek world. The Urartians had sensed the possibilities of this northern route. The Persians had kept their eyes on it, though they were more interested in tribute than in commerce. Now came the enterprising Greeks. Greek trading settlements and Greek culture spread all across eastern Asia Minor and, according to Pliny, "right up to the borders of mountainous Armenia." The Seleucid governor Patrocles traveled in person to Armenia, with a corps of engineers, to see if a canal could be dug to link the Black Sea with the Caspian Sea, three hundred miles away. He decided that it couldn't.

After the Greeks came the Romans. For the most part, the Greeks, like the Persians, had let the Armenians pretty much rule themselves. Now, with the rise of Rome, as the competing powers pushed and shoved each other across Asia Minor, the Armenians declared themselves independent, grabbed off some land from the long-downtrodden Medes, and announced that their satraps were now kings. One of the first of these, King Artaxias I, determined to erect a proper capital, which he called Artaxata—"the joy of Artaxias." It was laid out on the great green plain of Ararat by no less a surprise city planner than the retired Carthaginian general Hannibal. Plutarch wrote some years afterward, "Hannibal the Carthaginian, after the defeat of Antiochus by the Romans, coming to Artaxias, King of Armenia . . . observing the great natural capacities and pleasantness of the site, then lying unoccupied and neglected, drew a model of a city for it. . . . At which the King, being pleased, and desiring him to oversee the work, erected a large and stately city." Juvenal, the Roman satirist, later spoke of "the dissident morals of Artaxata," which is an intriguing notion.

For a while, the Romans and the Armenians maintained

a distant, amicable—or, at least, standoffish—relationship, but it wasn't likely that the Romans would ignore forever the strange lights of Artaxata winking away into the darkness on the periphery of the civilized world. For one thing, by the first century B.C. the Romans had become engaged in what would be one of history's most endless and pointless rivalries—that with Parthia, an Iranian federation, which had replaced the Achaemenid empire—and were therefore continually made aware of the strategic factor of Armenia. For another, the Romans, ever businesslike, were attracted to the possibilities of East-West trade, and, what with southeastern Asia Minor generally in turmoil, they became increasingly interested in the Armenian trade route. At one point, the Roman Senate sent the great general Pompey off to Armenia to chart a better passageway to India. Pompey traveled around Armenia and the Caucasus for a while, presumably trying to imagine a Roman thoroughfare through the Hindu Kush, and then recommended much the same route that already existed—except for the addition of a road to Trebizond (where Xenophon and his men had reached the sea), which was later built by Roman engineers. Like it or not, the Armenians were getting—or finding themselves —*involved*.

THERE IS ALSO the story of Tigran II of Armenia, known to Armenians as Tigran the Great. Tigran was a descendant of King Artaxias and became king of Armenia in 95 B.C., at a time when Rome was occupied elsewhere. He succeeded his father, Artavazd I, after paying a ransom of "seventy valleys" to the powerful Parthians, who had held him hostage for several years. Then Tigran murdered a neighboring Armenian prince and took over his territory. He next made an alliance with Mithridates, a warrior king who ruled the nearby country of Pontus, and married Mithridates' daughter Cleopatra (a different Cleopatra). In the name of his father-in-law, Tigran invaded the sizable kingdom of Cappadocia. The Roman general Sulla was called in and threw him out, but Tigran nevertheless went on to invade Parthia, where he got back his seventy valleys, and overran four Parthian vassal states. Having avenged himself against his former captors, he marched his army as far as the kingdom of Cilicia, which bordered the Mediterranean. He advanced into Syria and was presented with the Seleucid crown. Finally, he invaded Cappadocia again, this time successfully. By the year 70 B.C., Tigran of Armenia was the most powerful ruler in western Asia. The "Armenian empire" extended from the Ararat Valley, in the north, to the Mediterranean, in the south, and as far as Tyre, on the formerly Phoenician coast. Tigran called himself "King of Kings" and decreed that a new and greater Armenian capital should be built near the headwaters of the river Tigris, in central Asia Minor. Ah, Tigran! What a ferocious and unlovely old roughneck he must have been! Nor were his imperial pretensions without a certain dreadful style. It was his ambition to Hellenize his rougher countrymen, by colonizing the wild mountain lands of Armenia with settlements of cultivated Greeks. Alas, few cultivated Greeks wished to move into the mountains of Armenia—not even to Tigranocerta, the fine new city that Tigran was building on their southern edge. Tigran marched them there anyway: about three hundred thousand Greek prisoners from Cappadocia and Cilicia packed overland to the still building capital. A few came willingly: Amphicrates, an Athenian writer; also Metrodorus of Scepsis, who became a kind of resident historian to the monarch. The Roman writer Appian described Tigranocerta as "surrounded by a wall fifty cubits high, the base of which was full of stables," and he noted, "In the suburbs he built a palace and laid out large parks, hunting grounds, and lakes." A band of Greek actors (they were also prisoners) was in residence, preparing an entertainment for the inauguration of a new theater. Unfortunately, just before that happy event, the Romans arrived. The Greek geographer Strabo wrote, "Lucullus, who had waged war against Mithridates, arrived before Tigran had completed his undertaking, and not only dismissed the inhabitants to their several homelands but also attacked and utterly demolished the city, which was still only half finished, leaving a small village in its place."

Poor Tigran! But he did not give up so easily. He and Mithridates tried to drive off the Romans. When that didn't work, he seems to have turned on his father-in-law and erstwhile ally and attempted to have him murdered. Finally, a unique combination of Romans and Parthians subdued

Tigran sufficiently for him to surrender to Pompey, who had taken over from Lucullus. According to Plutarch, the Roman general received Tigran graciously, and allowed him to keep what little kingdom he had left, asking only that he pay a "fine" of six thousand talents. Then the old king went back north to Armenia—the original, unexpanded, unimperial Armenia—where he ruled for ten more years as a sort of vassal of the Romans, and in 55 B.C., at the age of eighty-five and dotty, he died in his sleep in Artaxata. Doubtless the quiet sleep of ferocious old men.

Tigran, our national hero! Tigran the Great! Presumably every nation must have its own Napoleon—one of those fascinating egomaniacs, with their *gloire,* and *Blitzkrieg* empires, and dead bodies all the way back from Moscow or Cappadocia—and perhaps it is better to have one fading in the scrapbook from two thousand years ago than pinkly smiling from the turret of a tank. I think with surprise, My father's name was Tigran—for surely that is a transliteration of Dikran, his first name and a common name among Armenians. Tigran smiling from the turret of a tank! Tigran among the nightingales! Ah, but I feel there was something about that old Tigran—perhaps such *ungentleness.*

Fresno, California: *"Fresno"* is a Spanish word meaning "ash tree." There are still some ash trees here, scattered far out of town, but the Spanish influence, as they call it, is pretty well gone by now, unless you count the roadside Margarita places and Taco Pete's. The Armenian presence is a little more visible, but not much. There are two Armenian churches. An Armenian bakery. Two or three Armenian restaurants. There used to be an Armenian community—"Armenian Town"—but it has largely disappeared, torn up to make way for the new expressway and the shopping center. There is a Basque presence, also an Italian presence, and a Japanese presence, but mainly a Wasp presence, for this is a California town, a micro-city. "Fresno: Pop. 180,000," say the big green signs. What is going on here is agribusiness, which means the great earth factory of the San Joaquin Valley: untold acres of farmland, fruitland, vineland. Trees and vines and pastureland extending for miles between the invisible Pacific and the dimly visible Sierra: snowcapped blue mountains seen through a bluish haze. Over on the coast is Monterey—John Steinbeck's Cannery Row and Tortilla Flat. Here was William Saroyan's hot, flat valley filled with fruit and crops and poverty and life. "A man could walk four or five miles in any direction from the heart of our city and see our streets dwindle to land and weeds," Saroyan wrote in the nineteen-thirties. "In many places the land would be vineyard and orchard land, but in most places it would be desert land and the weeds would be the strong dry weeds of deserts. . . . Our trees were not yet tall enough to make much shade, and we had planted a number of kinds of trees we ought not to have planted because they were of weak stuff and would never live a century, but we had made a pretty good beginning. Our cemeteries were few and the graves in them were few. We had buried no great men because we hadn't had time to produce any great men, we had been too busy trying to get water into the desert." I don't know what I expected it to be like now. I know not like that, because nothing is like that any more—certainly not in California. I think I expected to see Armenian faces at the airport or on the street. I think I expected to walk off the plane and see Armenians hanging around the car-rental counters, behind the car-rental counters. Armenians—for it was our town, wasn't it?

I stood one afternoon in a field on the outskirts of the city and looked at the fruit trees, which were bare in the March wind, and looked at the grapevines, which were also bare—brown tendrils close to the brown soil, stretching out to the horizon as far as the eye could see. The man who owned the field was an Armenian named Gadalian. He had

thick, graying hair and a wide, leathery face and thick
hands. He was about fifty years old, but an outdoor fifty—
square shoulders and a large, tough belly. He was worrying
about frost. "The frost is strange here," he said. "It comes in
waves across the valley. In one place there may be frost, but
on the farm across the road there may be no frost. Look at
this." He held up a grapevine that had been bent or broken
around another vine. "Nobody knows how to work the
vines any more," he said. It was a modest farm, about eighty
acres. There was a comfortable small farmhouse on the edge
of the property, just off the dirt road, with grapefruit trees in
the front and a kennel for two or three large dogs in the
back. We were standing next to a ramshackle old house or
hut of dark redwood, weathered by rain and sun—a place
for tools and empty boxes. "My father lived here," said
Gadalian, pointing inside. "This is where we grew up. He
was a good man, my father. He worked very hard."

My father committed no crime. The bare trees stretch
out everywhere. Bare branches against the metallic gray sky.
Plums. Peaches. Apples. Grapefruit. Grapes. Fertility. The
bluish mountains swim in haze against the sky.

"Did you know the Armenians brought the melons to
California?" said Gadalian. "The melon they call the Per-
sian melon. The casaba melon, whose seeds come from
Kasaba, in Turkey. Most of the melons in this valley were
grown by Arakelian. They called old Arakelian the Melon
King."

"Where is he?" I asked.

"He is dead, I think. Anyway, his sons have moved to Los Angeles."

"Are there many Armenians here?" I asked.

"There are some," he said. "There are not too many any more."

We stood beside stacks of empty raisin crates. Old boxes, weathered like the hut.

"Look at this one," said Gadalian, pointing to a box so old that its sides had started to split apart. "This one goes back to my father's time. Look at the way they made the corners."

"How is it your father came here?" I asked.

"I don't know," said Gadalian. Then, "I think he and my mother came from the old country around 1900, some time like that. For a while, they were in the East, around Worcester, Massachusetts. They worked in the shoe factories. There were a number of Armenians who worked in the shoe factories. Then they heard about California, where they could grow things."

"Was your father happy here?" I asked.

Gadalian seemed puzzled. "I don't know," he said. "It is hard to tell if a father is happy." Then, "He worked very hard. I remember that."

Little farms scattered around the great valley. These were some of the names on mailboxes: Pirogian, Kavanessian, Agajanian. A sign on an abandoned warehouse: "SIMOJIAN RAISINS, THE FINEST IN THE WORLD." I thought of Bud and his tropical fish in New York. I thought of my father, who had journeyed to Hollywood a number of times in his career but never to Fresno. What was here in Fresno? What had been here?

I thought of the simple warmth of a Saroyan story: "Walking along Alvin Street he felt glad to be home again. Everything was fine, common and good, the smell of earth, cooking suppers, smoke, the rich summer air of the valley full of plant growth, grapes growing, peaches ripening, and the oleander bush swooning with sweetness, the same as ever. . . . This valley, he thought, all this country between the mountains, is mine, home to me, the place I dream about, and everything is the same."

I thought, too, of what a friend of Gadalian's had said when I asked him where most of the Armenians in Fresno lived.

"Oh, now they can live anywhere," he said.

"What do you mean, anywhere?"

"There are no more restrictions," he said. "Before, it wasn't always so easy. Of course, you have to understand that a lot of the first Armenians here were country people. Farmers. Rough people." He smiled. He had enormous hands, fingers as thick as roots, palms caked with dirt. "They took away the restrictions at the end of the war," he said. And "This valley is my home. It's the place I dream about." Sometimes the dreams of people make one gasp.

AND NOW William Saroyan himself, standing in the lobby of the Fresno Hilton. William Saroyan at sixty-six. The hair thick but graying. A burly man. Stocky. A fine mustache. Also large hands. A laugh. Good eyes, a good face.

"I was out in the country," I said.

"It's beautiful, isn't it? You should come back in the summer," said Saroyan. "Of course, it is terrible in the summer. You sweat all day long. But then everybody is busy."

We drove through side streets, past the sterile glass office buildings of the new downtown, past the immense modern convention center. "Everything has changed," said Saroyan. "But of course it has changed. Look at that shopping center. Nobody comes to it. Do you see that street? I used to deliver papers up and down that street. It was a good job, too. The paper was called the Fresno *Republican,* and it was edited and published by Mr. Chester Rowell. Both are gone now, though there's a statue of the paper's founder in Courthouse Square."

We drove under a viaduct over which the new expressway was being built. The land ahead of us was mostly desolate from the bulldozers, but here and there a few small frame houses remained. "I'd show you where I grew up, but they tore that down, too," said Saroyan. "I hope for their sake more people use the new expressway than use the shopping center."

"There don't seem to be very many Armenians around," I said.

"There are still a few," said Saroyan. "Maybe ten thousand in the valley. But the town has grown, and the Armenians sold their land and moved to the cities."

"What about you?" I asked.

"I got tired of knocking around too much. One day, I decided to come back. Once you like a place, you always like it."

We drove away from the little streets and little houses, and out past the familiar landmarks of modern California: the endless strip of car lots and Mexican restaurants and bowling alleys and garden-supply stores and farm-hardware warehouses and motels with banquet and convention facilities.

I thought of a story of Saroyan's that I'd read long ago, which began, "I don't suppose you ever saw a two-hundred-and-fifty-pound Filipino." It's hard to forget a story that begins that way. I had read that story in school, when my favorite writers were Ernest Hemingway, Robert Benchley, and William Saroyan: Hemingway because he was so sexy with those sleeping bags; Benchley because he was so funny; and Saroyan because nobody could write to a person (me) the way that William Saroyan wrote.

There was another story, which I'd read on the plane to California—a story called "Five Ripe Pears." It began like this: "If old man Pollard is still alive I hope he reads this because I want him to know I am not a thief and never have been. Instead of making up a lie, which I could have done, I told the truth, and got a licking. I don't care about the licking because I got a lot of them in grammar school. . . . The licking Mr. Pollard gave me I didn't deserve, and I hope he reads this because I am going to tell him why. I couldn't tell him that day because I didn't know how to explain what I knew. . . . It was about spring pears." It was not an important story, but it was a lovely story—a story with a voice. It made one think with a kind of pleasure that J. D. Salinger must have heard that voice, and Richard Brautigan, and Jack Kerouac, and all those writers of the personal sound, the flower-writers, the writers of our modern Era of Feeling.

"I'm glad you decided to find out about Armenians," said Saroyan. "They're a crazy people, you know. Or sometimes they seem that way. But they're a very simple people."

We drove on awhile. Saroyan talked about his children—a daughter in New York, a son in San Francisco. Family talk. He asked me about my wife and children, about my sister, about my work. I felt something surprisingly paternal in his voice. It was a strange, deep feeling, as if we had known each other all along, when in fact I had met Saroyan only once before, briefly, a few years ago in New York, and had called him in Fresno only a week earlier to arrange our meeting.

We stopped to have dinner at a roadside restaurant, a roadside Armenian restaurant called Stanley's. A nice place, too, with bright lights and the ubiquitous Olde Steake House furniture and a photograph of Mt. Ararat behind the cashier's desk.

"Sometime I hope you'll meet my Uncle Aram," said Saroyan. "He's eighty-two now, and a fine man. I've written a lot of stories about Aram. People would ask me, 'Are they true stories?' I'd always reply, 'Of course not. I am a writer. I make things up. I embellish.' But it's been hard to embellish Aram."

Saroyan began to tell some stories about his Uncle Aram in a loud, resonant voice. The waiter brought some Armenian bread and a bottle of wine, then shish kebab. Saroyan laughed as he spoke. I looked at him and thought, My father was sixty when he died; he would be seventy-nine now. I thought of my father's frailness, his thin elegance; it seemed like such a different presence.

"You know, your father was a fine man," Saroyan said, as if he were reading my mind.

"Did you think of him as an Armenian?" I asked.

"Of course I did," said Saroyan. "An Armenian can never not be an Armenian. But your father went about it differently. I think he had other things on his mind."

"What kind of things?"

"I don't know," said Saroyan. "The truth is, I didn't see him often. We were different. But we were also close. I can't quite explain it. I remember the first time I met him. It was just after the war. I heard he was in New York, and I was passing through, and so I telephoned. We met at some hotel—the Hampshire House, or maybe the Pierre. I remember how we embraced; that is what I remember. Another time, this was a few years later, we had dinner at that restaurant—did you ever go?—the Golden Horn, and afterward we went back to where I was living. I had an apartment that winter on Central Park West. We talked about writing and families, I remember. Your father was about to start another book; at least, that is what he said, although I guess he never finished it. But it was a close time. I remember him standing in the corridor and looking in on our children, who were sleeping. The children were very young and they kept stirring in their sleep, and your father kept saying 'Shhh,' the way fathers do."

I thought of that photograph in the Golden Horn. The two comrades, the two Armenian writers—both of them in fact then passing the peak of their fame, my father putting on a graceful front of having "retired," Saroyan both more and less fortunate in not being able to retire but, instead, turning out a stream of novels and plays that critics were beginning to say did not compare to the early work.

A waitress came over to Saroyan with a menu she wished him to autograph. Saroyan signed it with a flourish and then asked her to sign one for him.

"I will tell you," Saroyan said to me. "If you want to know about Armenians, then you must go to Armenia, or what remains of it. You must go to Erevan—in Soviet Armenia."

"Have you been there?" I asked.

"Yes, I've been there. I went there the first time I earned any money. This was in 1935, and it wasn't much money, either. I went to New York and took one of those beautiful ships they had then. The *Berengaria*. I went to Europe and then to Soviet Armenia. They didn't have much in Armenia in those days, but it was a trip I had to make. I went back once again, in 1960."

"What did you find out when you went there?" I asked.

"I found out that there was an Armenia," said Saroyan. "Of course, it isn't what it used to be, but it *is* there; it is something."

We went back to Saroyan's house: a small tract house on one of the new streets—a modest house, on a street lined with perhaps a hundred similar houses. Inside, there was an extraordinary jumble of objects: not so much a disorder as a plenitude of things—books, and cartons, and suitcases, and boxes of this and that. In a large room off the kitchen, a tiny portable typewriter stood in the middle of a table piled with books and paper and manuscript. "I've always worked, and so I work now," said Saroyan. "Besides, I have to live."

"What are you writing?" I asked.

"I mostly write plays now. Sometimes people want to produce them, sometimes they do not. But that is what I do. Besides, my writing is better than my painting." He pointed to innumerable bright-colored abstract designs that had been pinned or Scotch-taped to the walls. Then he bent down in front of a pile of dusty magazines and pulled one out. "Did you ever see this?" he said. It was a copy of an old English-language Armenian magazine. Saroyan opened it to a picture of my father; in fact, it was a reproduction of a photograph that had appeared on a cover of *Time* in 1927—

now with a short note beside it on the "popular Anglo-Armenian novelist, formerly Dikran Kouyoumjian." Saroyan held the magazine open for a moment, and then put it down on the table. "It's a good photo of him, isn't it?" he said. "Such confidence."

"How is it that he never wrote anything serious about Armenians?" I asked.

"I think he wasn't that kind of writer," Saroyan said. "He liked to be entertaining. He made a couple of good jokes about Armenians, as I remember."

"Yes," I said. "But how is it that you wrote all the time about Armenians and he never did?"

"I don't know," said Saroyan. "Except that we all go on different journeys. Just like you. Now you come here. And soon, I think, you must go to Erevan."

We stood in the semidarkness of Saroyan's small house, surrounded by the clutter, the books, the magazines, the cartons, the jars of "treasures" that Saroyan had picked up on his travels or on the street. "I am a writer," Saroyan said. "It is something to be a writer. All my life, I have written. Also talked and drunk and gambled and everything else." He laughed. "They say that Armenians live to be very old. Did you know that? My grandmother Lucy Saroyan died at eighty-eight. My father's kid brother Mihran died at eighty. Come on. Let's go and look at the graveyard."

It was now midnight, or a bit later. We got in the car and drove through the silent streets of Fresno. It was hard to tell in which direction we were going—out toward the country or in toward the downtown. Darkened houses flicked by in the night. "It is too bad you don't know Armenian," Saroyan said. "Although you will survive. But it is a marvelous language—marvelous sounds. Do you know their songs? I shall sing one for you."

Saroyan sang, rolling down the window of the car. Outside, it had begun to rain—one of those fine, sprinkling nighttime rains. Saroyan's voice filled the car, the countryside silent except for the sound of our tires on the wet road. "It is a song about love and injustice and about pomegranates getting ripe," said Saroyan. "In other words, about the important things in life."

The car stopped beside the road. "Come on," he said, getting out. The rain was pouring down more heavily, but the air was warm and had a kind of fragrance. "Now, over there is the Protestant graveyard," he said. "And somewhere down there are the Catholics. And right here are the Armenians." Saroyan was wearing an old hat, a kind of old newspaperman's hat—a hat from *The Time of Your Life,* maybe. Now he began to run at a trot through the graveyard. We passed dim gravestones in the darkness. "Over there is Levon!" he called. "I think one of Lucy's sisters is here!" The grass was soft and slippery underfoot. Saroyan kept up a steady jog. "I think somewhere over there is Uncle Mirhan!" He stopped, breathing heavily. "You know, everybody seems the same in a graveyard—Protestant, Catholic, and Armenian. But still there is something different. I don't know what it is." He wiped his forehead, which was damp with rain and sweat. "Come on," he said. "It's wet here. It's time to go home."

Later on, when we said goodbye, Saroyan embraced me. I could feel his rough cheek scrape against mine. His rough, robust cheek. "Fathers and sons are always different," he said. "But they are also the same. Maybe you will find out about that, too. Anyway, I was truly fond of him and now I am fond of you, and that is something, is it not?" He clasped my hand, and put the newspaperman's hat back on his head, and tugged his jacket about him more closely, for a cold wind was blowing now, and stuffed his hands in his pockets, and turned back to the car, and got in and drove away across "the valley full of plant growth, grapes growing, peaches ripening, and the oleander bush swooning with sweetness," to the house with the cartons and suitcases and the small portable typewriter.

I watched him go, still feeling the roughness of his face against mine.

And so, in due course, I journeyed to Armenia—
to Soviet Armenia, or what should be called more precisely
the Armenian Soviet Socialist Republic. Armenia *is* there,
Saroyan had said. All right, I thought, I will go see it. The
passage was not simple to arrange, nor was it extremely difficult. I was told there was a Cultural Commitee in Soviet
Armenia, which might be interested in sponsoring such an
expedition. There were letters to be written, and officials to
be seen at the United Nations. The Soviet Russians were
brusque and noncommittal. The Soviet Armenians brought
a bottle of Armenian brandy in a paper bag into the U.N.
dining room, and discussed the New York Knicks, and said
that the matter would be "no problem." Three months later,
it was arranged.

From the start, I knew that it would be a complex
journey, a journey on many levels. At the least, it would be a
voyage within an adventure, for what could a trip of six
thousand miles be—even six thousand boring sky miles—but
an adventure? A flight into the past as well as a flight into
that even more startling region of the present—although
which past I would find, and whose present, it was hard to
tell. I was excited by the prospect of the trip, and also appre-

(5 5)

hensive about it. With a new anxiety, I realized that although for so many years I had gone without my Armenian background—had gone without it to the point of finally feeling deprived of it—at the same time its very vagueness in my life had been a form of protection: the remote familiarity of a dream. All my life, Armenia and Armenians had been part of a dream; it and they were *out there* somewhere, hazy, nearly invisible. Now I was traveling into the dream. I would see what I would see. I would find what I would find.

FLIGHT. Flying . . . flight. One May night, I rode with my wife above the lights of the world, above the clouds—two moderns, uncomfortably seated, covered (as if in protective layers) with newspapers and magazines and books, rushing in our stale-aired Aeroflot tube through the clear black night.

My wife dozed beside me, a copy of *Time* and a book of Byzantine history on her lap. Beneath her feet was a large satchel full of books about Armenia, which I had brought with us with a view to reading about Armenians "on location." I glanced at *Time,* which showed a painting of the French Premier on its cover. I thought of my father's youthful face on that *Time* cover long ago. In truth, I never thought his face changed much with the years. It was always somehow *set.* "Your father is a very thoughtful man," my mother once said to me. I wondered what he would make of my embarking on this trip. I thought, without quite knowing why, that he would dislike me for it.

I remembered then a dream I had had the previous night —our last, restless night in New York. In fact, it was a recurring dream, which I had dreamed many times in my youth. I could not recall having dreamed it since I was twenty-five or so, though—which, as it happened, was around the time my father died. The dream was this: We are in France and I am a child. My father and I drive down a sunlit road. There are tall trees on either side. Green fields. There is a fork in the road, and we take the turn marked "TO THE AIRPORT." I remember the airport well, for it was a real airport. Small, nineteen-thirties airplanes—aeroplanes. A grass runway. A red wind sock. A large blue plane stands in the middle of the runway, and my father walks toward it. He climbs the steps to the doorway and then stands and motions for me to follow. I come across the grass, running. But as I reach the top step he goes inside. I stand on the top step and stick my head inside. There all is darkness. *Black*. I have never seen such empty darkness as in that dream airplane I peer into, and then, somehow, I am standing on the grass again, the wind is blowing, and the blue plane is gone.

It had always been an unsettling dream for me, full of sunlight and terror. I wondered why I had dreamed it again so recently. In the stillness of our speeding jet, I gripped my wife's hand. She stirred but stayed asleep. Inside the cabin, there was a dim glow of light; the elbows of Russian businessmen were visible in the seats in front of me. Outside was another blackness, the darkness of the starless night sky. For one feeble moment, I wished myself back in time, back on the ground, back even to that country road long ago—the tall trees, the fields, the green everywhere, the two of us in that car. I wondered why each time we took the turnoff to the airport. What had been on the other road?

Half asleep, I looked out into the night and saw my father's face looking in, squinting, trying to see something. I sat up. But, of course, it was my own face, my reflection in the glass, squinting, trying to see something, looking out.

Now LET ME say something of Mt. Ararat, for visibly there was a Mt. Ararat, which we glimpsed in early morning, standing far off, across the Turkish border, perhaps fifty miles away—a clear, bright early morning, with the gold sunlight glinting off the airplane's wing, and off the blue-white snow of Ararat. It was an uncommon sight. I had had no expectation that it would be the way it was. After all, how many of those wretched paintings had I seen in recent months, with their garish colors and "important" perspectives? What had I expected it to look like? It doesn't matter. Having grown up, one learns to diminish childhood legends: the oak tree in one's grandmother's garden is still there thirty years later, but it is always smaller, less substantial, *less*. How could it be otherwise (one thinks), and how could we have made up all those stories about it? But Ararat was *more*. One part of my mind, perhaps my Anglo-American mind, told me that its special presence—for truly it possessed a special presence, standing off against the horizon: enormous, by itself—was due to a trick or chance of geology. For, unlike most large mountains, it did not rise out of foothills or appear to be part of a contiguous range. Ararat was in fact two peaks: a smaller one attached to a much greater one—Ararat proper—which, as I knew, reached a height of some seventeen thousand feet. But the Ararat massif, as it was called, stood there alone: a gigantic pyramid or Mayan temple rising from the flat plain into our sky. And the other part of my mind felt a deep shiver, perhaps what an archaeologist might feel at uncovering some such towering ancient monument, some *god,* and realizing (even within his modern soul) that it was a god, and that men in distant times had surely prayed to it, had looked with joy and terror on its blank face, had lived beneath it, doubtless feeling a deeper shiver, creating legends and demigods around it. Inevitably, the Ark! Where else?

A burly Russian businessman rose and leaned across the seats behind us and pointed to the great mountain, which we were now banking away from. "Mt. Ararat," he said. "It is beautiful, no?"

We nodded. Yes.

"The Americans have radar on the back of it," he said, and he gave a short, brusque laugh and sat down.

"What did he mean?" my wife asked me.

"He meant that Turkey is part of NATO," I said.

"It seems so sad that the Armenians don't own Ararat any more," she said.

"You can't *own* a mountain like that!" I said, with a vehemence that surprised us both.

She looked at me a moment as she bent to pack the books back into the satchel. "What a curious thing to say," she said. Then, "You know, I could swear you had tears in your eyes when you saw that mountain."

"I didn't," I said angrily. And "I'm not one of those Returning Sons."

And then we landed.

Erevan: The capital of Soviet Armenia, and once the site of the northernmost Urartian fortress, Erebuni. According to the tourist brochures (simple, amateurishly printed little handbooks), it was now a city of some seven hundred thousand people, and certainly the tourist brochures appeared to be right, for on all sides of us stretched broad avenues, narrow streets, modest dwellings, offices, a few shops, and large numbers of people. It was a city within a semicircle of hills. New apartment buildings jutted up everywhere. Mostly, they were a chalky pink—pink stone blocks of buildings. Building blocks. These were neither truly graceful nor as stark and harsh as buildings I had seen in other Communist countries. The concrete blockhouses I'd once glimpsed in Moscow had seemed a kind of nightmare. There appeared to be no similar nightmare in Erevan.

May. Springtime. But it was hot. A hot haze everywhere. A haze covered the hills, which were surely leaf green but seemed a shade of olive. The sky was a faded blue. We were in the center of the town, and there was a mass of people all around us. A mass of people on the sidewalks. A mass of people filling the small parks. Suddenly I knew where we

were: in a Balkan capital—a nameless Balkan capital, with
dust in the air, and car exhaust fumes in the street (for there
were cars everywhere), and an aura of being neither very
poor nor very rich. Men in loose-fitting black suits, or else in
shirtsleeves, lounged against the sides of buildings. Men
played chess on benches beneath the dust-covered trees.

Men! I realized that they were all Armenian. I was in a
city where virtually everybody was Armenian. For if there
had been a number of square-faced, burly, blondish Russians
on the airplane, they had since vanished, perhaps into some
Russian *quartier,* or else into a cluster of ponderous, clearly
official red brick buildings we had passed on our way in
from the airport. Everywhere, now, were dark faces, dark
hair, dark eyes—the faces not exactly dark in skin color but
dark, rather, in some feeling or expression. Armenians!

OUR HOTEL was oddly gracious, or almost gracious: a
large, old-fashioned place, also built out of the ubiquitous
pink stone, and fronting on the central square. Lenin
Square, although, apart from the predictable and rather
modest statue of Himself—not in the middle of it, either, but
off to one side—there were few signs of Soviet style either
outside the hotel or within it. There was the standard Soviet
watch-lady on our floor, but she had a classic Armenian face.
An ample, dark-haired woman seated upon a wicker chair,
looking at television.

Our room was also large and old-fashioned: the usual

bedroom and, in addition, a studio room—doubtless provided by the Cultural Committee—containing some simple wooden furniture and a piano. I sat for a moment in a chair in our room. Our room with the piano—our room in Armenia. Oh, I had mixed feelings. I knew not which.

We went out onto the street. There was a small park near the hotel. An ice-cream stand at the entrance. A bootblack with an elaborate "customer's chair," made out of leather and brass, each part of it finely polished and shining in the sun. Inside the park there were more men playing chess, and children swinging on a half-dozen swings. The children with large brown eyes. Armenian children! It was a gay scene, a summer's scene. The dust from the dirt paths rose beneath our feet. Children's laughter sounded in the leaves. I wanted to embrace them—to embrace somebody. But I could not. A voice inside me spoke: You have come this far. You must make a connection. But I could not. I knew, too, that it was a question not of my having to rush and embrace some stranger—for my temperament always stopped me short of such gestures—but only of my *feeling* something: of feeling real warmth as opposed to the pale heat of (in this case) literary sensibility. Old men and children in a park! A summer's scene! An Armenian scene! But I felt frozen.

"Now, *there's* an Armenian!" I heard my wife say.

I looked where she had been looking—toward a group of people gathered around some chess players. On the outside of the group were some young men, perhaps in their early twenties. One of them stood out from all the rest: tall, curly-haired, quite fiercely handsome. I knew which one she meant, but I said, "Who?"

My wife laughed. She was easily made shy. "Oh," she said. "You know which one." Now she was embarrassed. "The one with the blue shirt. Isn't he striking?"

I looked at him again. Yes, he was striking. He was a fine young man. But somehow I felt incapable of replying, of responding. It was quite startling. I knew that it wasn't on account of some simple jealousy—it didn't seem to have much to do with *him*. It was as if I had been found out in something—something that had to do with how *I* cared about the way Armenians looked, and that I couldn't bear to admit.

Just then, a voice behind me said, in English, "I thought I'd find you here. It is a lovely park, is it not?"

We turned to see a square-shouldered man in a brown suit—a man of medium build, of medium age, with a hard Armenian face, which seemed to be smiling.

"Permit me to introduce myself," he said. "I am Sarkis. I am not your guide. Your guide is an excellent young man who is always occupied. I am your friend." He paused, then stepped forward and shook my wife's hand in a vigorous and awkward grip, and then threw his arms around me in an embrace. "Welcome to Armenia!" he said.

How to describe this Sarkis, who had arrived apparently from nowhere, and who now walked beside us—a bustling, short-legged figure in a brown suit (an unusually warm brown suit for the season), gesticulating, talking? Our friend? In reality, the mystery of his appearance soon became less mysterious, yet it was still fascinating, for, although neither officially a guide nor precisely an interpreter, he was in private life a teacher, a teacher of English at a local high school, who maintained, as he put it, "connections" with the Cultural Committee, and who periodically offered his services to visitors—to sympathetic visitors.

"I knew right away that you would be sympathetic," he said as we walked across the street toward the central square. "Besides, you are Armenian. All Armenians are sympathetic to one another, are they not?"

I nodded. I could see my wife smiling, walking lightly. She was pleased that we had found a friend—at least, a "personal contact," not one of those mechanical guides we had dreaded. It occurred to me that she liked Armenians better than I did.

"Is your father still living?" Sarkis asked me.

I said no.

"I understand he was a writer, also," Sarkis said. "Unfortunately, I have never read his work. Did he ever travel to Soviet Armenia?"

"He never did," I said.

"What a pity," Sarkis said. "I am sure he would have liked it. He would have admired the achievements of the Armenian people."

"Yes, I'm sure he would have," I said.

Sarkis turned to my wife. "Did you know his father?"

"No, I didn't," she said. "I wish I had."

"I am sure he was a wonderful man," said Sarkis. "Armenian men make wonderful fathers. They worship their families. They would do anything for their families."

We stood now in the middle of the square, beside some fountains. I thought, Why won't this man stop about my father—about fathers, Armenian fathers? I knew it was a childish thought, and disliked myself for thinking it, and Sarkis for making me think it.

My wife apparently noticed a new expression on my face. "What's the matter?" she asked.

Sarkis overheard. In some ways, he was obviously very agile. "Is something the matter?" he said. "Probably you are tired after your long voyage. Forgive me for talking so much, but in these parts one rarely has a chance for such international conversation."

He was so singular and charming I couldn't imagine what anger, or peevishness, had possessed me. "I think it's mostly hunger," I said.

We walked over to our hotel.

"You have lunch," said Sarkis. "I have some business to attend to. Afterward, I am going to take you somewhere very special."

My wife and I found a table in the hotel restaurant—a large, high-ceilinged room crowded with customers and waiters (Armenian customers! Armenian waiters!), all of them speaking not Russian but Armenian. A beaming waiter presented an enormous menu with virtually all the items crossed out. We ordered a dried-beef dish, some kind of greenish salad, and a white wine. Four men at a nearby table were drinking brandy and singing—a soft and almost dainty melody.

Once again, everything seemed gay though somehow oppressive. My wife talked excitedly of her impressions of the new city. I felt myself silent, trying to listen, trying to listen to everything.

"What happened to you out there?" she asked.

"It was nothing," I said.

"Was it all that about your father?"

"Perhaps that was a bit of it," I said. "I don't know why."

"But Armenians always go on like that," she said. "You told me so yourself. You mustn't mind it."

"I know," I said. Then, because it was what I felt, I said, "You know, I don't think I really *like* Armenians."

"You know you don't mean that," she said. She smiled. Beside us, the singing rose into a kind of march. The waiters clapped their hands. We had more wine and finished off the greenish salad, which was mostly scallions, with a kind of bitter, pungent taste.

Sarkis reappeared outside. He was in command of an ancient Russian touring car, a definitely imposing vehicle of unnamed manufacture and of vaguely czarist inclinations: faded limousine upholstery, remains of a lap-robe cordon in the back (without the lap robe), and little, tattered curtains on the side windows, bespeaking a romantic past of modest bureaucratic trysts or kidnappings, or both.

"Naturally, it is not mine," said Sarkis, seeming very pleased. "I have borrowed it from the Committee. Naturally, it belongs to the State."

"I had hoped it was Armenian—an Armenian car," my wife said.

"I do not think so," said Sarkis. Then, "You are not joking?"

"No, I wasn't," she said.

"Armenians make many valuable things now in Armenia," said Sarkis. "In America, how do you call them—products? Armenians make electrical products. They make computers. Armenians make excellent computers. Look!" He pointed to a cloud of dark smoke on the horizon. "You call that pollution, but we are still poorer than you. We call it industry."

"Are we going to a factory now?" I asked, for I had come prepared to visit many factories.

"No," said Sarkis. "Not today. The Committee will arrange for you to visit factories. Today, on your arrival, I am taking you on a special trip—to a place that all Armenians would want to visit. I am taking you to a *hallowed* place. We call it the Monument—the Monument to the Armenian Martyrs."

We climbed into the front seat of the limousine, squeezed in beside Sarkis, who handled the old machine with a classic pedagogic mixture of vagueness and speedway fervor. "I do not drive very often," he said disarmingly, "although I had a motorcycle for many years."

It didn't seem right to inquire what had happened to the motorcycle.

We drove down one of the wide boulevards, a long, straight roadway lined with trees, which led toward the semicircle of low hills.

The olive-colored leaves were deep green as we came closer. There were flowers beside the road, and a few houses. It seemed suddenly as if we were in a different country—as if we had left the Balkans behind us in the dusty city and were now motoring through some more familiar minor bit of Europe. There were orange-tiled roofs on the poorish stone houses, red flowers in the skimpy gardens. Some goats wandered beside the road.

Then even this feeling of Europe died out. Meadows of yellow-green grass extended on all sides. The fields were flat and dry and full of stones. You could see clusters of trees against the horizon, far away, and a few scattered houses, far away—and, yet farther away, the mass of Ararat, not quite in front of us but dominating the land, its summit of snow on a level with the clouds.

"Every Armenian in the world should visit this monument," Sarkis was saying. "Every Armenian should know what it is to stand before it and feel in his bones the tragedy of Armenia." He turned to my wife. "The suffering of the

Armenian people has been enormous," he said. "Enormous. Incomprehensible. Are you acquainted with the suffering of the Armenian people?"

"I've read something about it," she said. "It seemed truly terrible."

"Ah, you've read about it," he said. "Your husband must be a good Armenian. He understands that it is necessary for us to speak out about these things." With one hand he reached out and clasped my arm. "Have you told her what happened at Van and Bitlis? Have you told her how the Turks clubbed our poor people to death? Have you told her how they tortured our men and raped our women?" He turned to my wife. "Did you know, my dear, that they burned priests on crosses and killed small infants with their bayonets? Yes, that is right. Small infants. They killed small children with their knives and bayonets. Oh, it was surely horrible, the most horrible of deeds."

I was conscious of the dry straw of the fields floating past us. Sarkis stared straight ahead. Ararat was a dream.

Sarkis said, "To be an Armenian is to have this intolerable weight of sadness on one's soul. That is what one of our Armenian poets said. Is it not true?"

In a moment, he said, "Armenians can never forget what happened to them. Armenians must never forget. It was a genocide. Do you know, it was the world's first genocide."

It seemed as if we drove for hours, but it was less than one hour. The heat was everywhere. There were no people—

only yellow fields shimmering in the sun. Sarkis stopped the car—our destination.

We climbed some stone steps. There was a stone walk. "You should take off your coat," Sarkis said. I took off my coat. I felt oddly grateful that he had said that. In front of us, about a half mile away, was an unusual structure. It had the appearance of a kind of Stonehenge—columns, metallic columns rising out of the ground, but angled inward. A Stonehenge of slanted slabs.

"How beautiful!" I could hear my wife saying. "How extraordinary!"

"Of course it is beautiful," Sarkis said. He walked just a step in front of us. For some reason, I was conscious of his stride—a stolid, heavy gait—and of his belly, which seemed not so much fat as hard, a politician's belly.

Suddenly he stooped down and plucked a little flower from the grass beside the walk. He looked at me. "For our Armenian martyrs," he said.

I was conscious of his eyes on me, my wife's eyes on me. On all sides of us I could see fields stretching away into the distance. I knew there were flowers beneath my gaze, but I could see no flowers. I kept on walking.

In the center of the slanted columns stood a large vessel—a metal bowl—with a flame burning inside it.

We stood beneath the columns looking at the bowl and the flame.

"Think of the Armenians who died," said Sarkis, almost

in a whisper. "Think of your martyred countrymen. Think what it is to be an Armenian."

Sarkis's voice was only a murmur, but it seemed to roar in my ears. I knew that I felt nothing. An image flickered through my mind of soldiers in a First World War movie advancing in slow motion across a muddy field, being mown down in slow motion by machine-gun fire, turning, falling, falling in silence. Sarkis reached out toward me and put the flower he had been holding into my hand.

"I saved this for you," he said. "For your offering."

I looked at him. "I can't," I said.

For a moment, we looked at one another. I could find no meaning in his glance or mine.

"Please . . ." my wife said.

The flower—it was a kind of buttercup, I think—was in my palm. I took a few steps forward and placed it—gently dropped it—in the flaming bowl. And turned and began to walk back slowly, away from the bowl and out from beneath the overhanging columns.

Sarkis and my wife were a step or so behind me, then beside me. They were talking about the Monument. "Each year in April," Sarkis was saying, "our people come down here from Erevan to bow their heads. Some of them even make the journey on foot."

I thought, I have come this far—so close—but I seem unable to go further, to make the connection.

Over my shoulder I glimpsed Ararat in the distance: a blue shape in a bluish haze. It seemed as silent as the dry fields, as the yellow flowers, as everything in sight. I thought quite simply, How strange to have no country. Just then, a breeze from somewhere rippled the fields. I heard my wife's laugh. The flowers swayed in the breeze from the blue mountain.

In the course of the next few days, I lived a curious interior life. That is, I stayed indoors whenever possible and read my books.

Even my wife thought it peculiar. "You've come all the way to Armenia and you won't go out and look around."

This wasn't entirely true, for we were not let off so easily, either by the official guide—a sober young bureaucrat named Vartan, who made an appearance daily, by phone if not in person, with a schedule of places (factories, schools, and churches) we should visit—or by Sarkis, who, far from being put off by my unresponsive manner at the Monument, persisted in his efforts to befriend us and to have some role in our visit.

But it was mainly true. For although I sometimes walked the dusty city and craned my neck at ancient churches, and though I sat through a performance of *Othello* (in Armenian, too) with Sarkis, I lived in those days mostly in the Armenian books I had brought, and in our rooms. I didn't even know for certain what it was I wanted to find out from these histories. I told myself, "Through the past I'll find the present"—or some such thing. At any rate, I read obsessively in the old volumes.

It continued to fascinate me that Armenia had had such a past, although the more I read, the less sure I was exactly what I meant by that—"such a past." From one point of view, Armenia existed throughout history largely as a footnote, a cluster of footnotes. In the classic texts on Persian history, Arab history, Byzantine history, and so forth, one would scan the index for Armenia, and there it would be: "Armenia: pp. 51–57; pp. 120–124; p. 237." And so forth. But from another point of view I knew that these footnotes were the murmurs of real people, real events. My people.

I was drawn to revelations of Armenians as soldiers, as warriors. For it seemed that the martial qualities recounted by Xenophon and the horsemanship once nurtured by the Persians had propelled many Armenians into the military foreground by the time of the Byzantines. For example, in Procopius's great history of Justinian's campaign for the recapture of Rome from the barbarians one might find the names of at least a dozen Armenian generals. There was the surreal and marvelous figure of old Narses: General Narses, also an Armenian, formerly the Grand Chamberlain (a high official in the Byzantine treasury), who at the age of seventy was appointed by Justinian to command the Imperial Army, which had been sent from Constantinople into the darkness of the Italian provinces to overthrow the Ostrogoth Totila. Narses had done it, too—killing Totila, and overwhelming the barbarians, who "immediately handed over themselves and the fortress," Procopius wrote. "In this way, Rome was taken for the fifth time in [Justinian's] reign, and Narses at once sent its keys to the Emperor." It seemed one of those eerie, dreamlike images that shine dimly through history—a point of light from a distant, receding star. Narses the Armenian, prefect of Italy.

What a curious people! Clearly, for hundreds of years Armenians had been among the key figures of the long-lasting Byzantine empire. They were generals. They were emperors. Consider Leo V (813–20). "As to his immediate origin, it is well known," wrote a contemporary historian, George the Monk. "He came from the country of the Armenians, whence, according to some, his obstinacy and his bad disposition." There was the dynasty started by the Emperor Basil I—originally a peasant, born in Macedonia of Armenian parents, who came to Constantinople at the age of twenty and "found favor" with the current emperor, then assisted the emperor by murdering a troublesome uncle, then murdered the emperor and took the job himself. Apparently, he made a good emperor, too—at least, the way historians like to view these things: a Byzantine "strong man," who fought off the Saracens and kept everybody in line. He increased the Army, maintained a sober interest in legal reform, and liked to wrestle after dinner.

For a while, Armenians must have been nearly everywhere in the imperial hierarchy. "The Armenian element was also prominent in the intellectual life of Byzantium, which underwent a notable revival in the ninth century," wrote D. M. Lang in *Armenia: Cradle of Civilization.*

"Prominent in this movement were such figures of part Armenian blood as John the Grammarian, Caesar Bardas, and Leo the Philosopher. . . . Also of partial Armenian descent was Patriarch Photius (820–93), whose stormy patriarchate marked the beginning of the schism between the Eastern and Western Churches."

For a while after the death of Basil I, a kind of triumvirate ruled the empire (still the most powerful political entity in the world)—two co-emperors and a general, *all* Armenian. And then, of course, there was Basil II—the last of the line. He was known at the time as Basil Bulgaroctonus, which means "slayer of Bulgars." For this reason: After a battle against the unfriendly Bulgars, whom he defeated, Basil ordered that the eyes of all fifteen thousand Bulgar prisoners should be put out save for every hundredth man, who should have only one eye put out, so that he could lead his blinded comrades home. It is said that the czar of the Bulgars, Samuel, died of a stroke at the sight of his returning army.

I COULDN'T HELP noticing how attracted I was to these terrible Armenians. First, Tigran the Great. Now the two Basils. Bulgaroctonus indeed! That was surely one of the least appealing stories I had ever read. Imagine how much time it must have taken to blind fifteen thousand men. Imagine the length of the line—imagine being the ninety-ninth man, or even the hundredth. Perhaps "attracted" is too strong a word. But certainly I was more than just aware of them.

Then, there was the interest I took in Armenian generals—the Armenian warrior spirit. I, who in my adult life had regarded myself as so devoutly anti-militarist! One afternoon, I read aloud to my wife a brief passage that I had uncovered in Procopius about John the Armenian, a commander of the Byzantine cavalry under Belisarius who by a brilliant ruse had won some North African battle against the Vandals.

Afterward, she said simply, "But what are you looking for? Of course the Armenians are brave."

"That's not the *point,*" I said. I didn't know what the point was.

ANOTHER TIME, my wife said, "Sarkis wants us to go to an art exhibit with him."

I said, "Can't you see that I'm in the middle of studying?" I thought that if I called it "studying" I would add dignity to my obsession. "Besides, there aren't any first-rate Armenian artists."

"I didn't know that," she said.

"You go," I said. "If the pictures are any good, you can tell me and I'll go later."

"All right," she said.

Instead of studying, I went by myself for a walk. It was a

terribly hot day; the dust was everywhere. I walked on the shady side of the street, close to the buildings. Nothing seemed cool. Women passed by carrying large, circular loaves of bread. Men stood silently in doorways. At the end of the street, there was an ice-cream vender, selling little cups of ice cream to children. I walked along and thought, Sarkis has been trying to *define* me as an Armenian—but a certain kind of Armenian. Those damned massacres, I thought. That chauvinism, such a chauvinism of misfortune!

Across the way there was a large, shedlike building with people going in and out of it. I went inside; it was an immense farmers' market. Sawdust on the floor. Heaps of vegetables on the counters. I thought to buy some oranges for our room, because there seemed to be no fruit available at the hotel. The man behind the orange counter was young: gold teeth, a peasant's face. After I'd paid him for six oranges, he put an extra orange on the pile. "Wilcom," he said. Welcome.

I thanked him, wanted to pay him more. He declined vigorously. I gave him a ball-point pen, which seemed to please him. Wilcom, wilcom.

On all sides, there were mountains of oranges. Radishes —flowery bursts of pink and green. The old women behind the counters wore shawls about their heads, wound like a veil across the lower face, and had the skin of elephants. Armenian women from the old country. Truly, here was the old country. I had never seen such women: the skin of elephants, the eyes of bears—old bears.

Later, as I walked back to the hotel, I thought, The man behind the orange counter had seen me as American. Do I, after all, look American? And so am I American?

When my wife returned, she seemed in good spirits. "The paintings weren't very good, but they do try so hard," she said. "We ran into one of Sarkis's students—a huge, bright young boy. At least, I think he was bright. We all had a lemonade together."

I read my book. I wanted to ask her if she thought I looked American or Armenian, or what? But it seemed a stupid question.

OUTSIDE THE POST OFFICE, one morning, I had a conversation with Sarkis about literature.

"Have you read the works of Abovian?" he asked.

"No, I haven't," I said. "Unfortunately, I haven't read many Armenian writers."

"That's too bad," he said. "We have some great writers."

"I know," I said.

"In addition to Abovian, we have Toumanian, Berberian, Isahakian, Aharonian, and, of course, Raffi. You have heard of Raffi?"

"Yes. But I haven't read any of them."

"That's too bad," he said. "But you have read Saroyan?"

"Yes, I've read Saroyan," I said.

"He is a great Armenian writer," said Sarkis. "Also a

great world writer. If you like, I will lend you some books by Abovian."

"That would be nice," I said.

Sarkis and I shook hands to go our own ways for the day. He paused. "Should I have included your father?"

"I don't know," I said. "It doesn't matter."

"It doesn't matter," Sarkis repeated. "You know, I wonder was he as detached as you." He smiled and waved and walked off across the square.

Back with my books, I became absorbed in the period of the Crusades. I knew that Armenia, in 301, had been the first nation in the world to officially adopt Christianity as a state religion, but I didn't know that Armenians had later become involved in the Crusades. It seemed so unlikely. Even my ignorance interested me. Before I left New York, an Armenian priest, who told me that I could never properly appreciate the "Armenian experience" without studying the Armenian role in the Crusades, had lent me several books. One (the shortest) was by an Armenian: *Cilician Armenia and the Crusades,* by Armen Ovhanesian. The others were a French work, the *Histoire des Croisades,* by René Grousset; and two volumes from the Englishman Steven Runciman's *A History of the Crusades.*

To begin with, there seemed some variance in bias about the Armenian role in the Crusades. The Armenians, not surprisingly, generally espoused the view that had been expressed long ago by Pope Gregory XIII: "Among the other merits of the Armenian nation as regards the Church and Christendom, there is one that is outstanding and deserves particularly to be remembered; namely, that when in past times the Christian princes and armies went forth to recover the Holy Land, no nation, no people came to their aid more

speedily and with more enthusiasm than the Armenians."
Scholars, on the whole, were less enthusiastic than the Pope,
although the French historians seemed mainly friendly toward the Armenian role. Grousset's book contained numerous references to the Armenians, especially in connection
with the First Crusade. This sort of thing: "As one sees in
many instances, the role of the native population was a vital
factor in the success of the Crusade . . . and indeed it was
the friendship between the Armenians and the Franks
which set the basis for the Latin Orient." The Armenian
author Ovhanesian quoted another French historian, Professor Joseph Laurent: "The Armenians guided and provi-
sioned the Crusaders. As signs of coöperation they [the
Armenians] married their daughters to them. They opened
to them the cities and fortresses from Tarsus to Marash,
from Samosata to Edessa. They made possible the capture of
Antioch, which foretold the capture of Jerusalem and the
success of the whole enterprise." The Englishman, Steven
Runciman, seemed coolest toward the subject. His books
acknowledged Armenian aid to the Crusaders: "As Baldwin
moved toward the river Euphrates, the Armenian population rose up to greet him," and so on. But his approach was,
in the modern, Lytton Strachey manner, a decidedly anti-
heroic treatment of the great European adventure: a rich
narrative of baronial mistrust, double-dealing, treachery, and
political feuding—activities in which the Armenians appeared to have participated as eagerly and recklessly as the
Crusaders.

One might well ask, What were the Armenians doing in this part of the world, on the Levant coast of Asia Minor, many hundreds of miles southwest of the Armenian plateau? The answer appeared to be that large numbers of Armenians had been driven from their homeland by increasing incursions of Seljuk Turks. Also, equally large numbers of Armenians—whole towns and counties, under individual barons or princes—had been resettled earlier by the Byzantine government to populate newly conquered territories. In addition to these displacements, until the eleventh century the defense of the Byzantine empire had been left mainly (and with relative success) to the national armies of the provincial territories, of which the Armenian was the second-largest in the empire, its borders forming the key frontier against the raiding Turks. The Byzantine government, however, in what was surely a classic example of bureaucratic wrongheadedness, decided to insure central control from Constantinople by dissolving the Armenian army, with the result that by the time of the first full-scale Seljuk invasion, in 1045, almost half the Armenians had moved off the Armenian plateau. Where had these Armenians moved to? They had migrated southwest to the next-best replica of their own mountainous terrain: to the craggy, lower, dark-green mountains of the Taurus and Amanus ranges, close by the Mediterranean coast of Cilicia, which country soon became known as Cilician Armenia.

The Arabs and the Turks were in this general area, too— at first, farther south and east. They were both Muslim. The

Armenians were militantly Christian, and since their conversion they had obdurately maintained their own branch of the Church. Then the Crusaders arrived: adventurous, belligerent, rather crude by Asia Minor standards, but also Christian. The Crusaders were short of food, of supplies, and of places to rest. The Armenians were at odds with the nearby Muslims as well as with the oppressive and distant Byzantines. Clearly, they looked to their new European friends as a counterweight to both. Such friends! In the beginning, most of the Crusaders were Frankish or Norman: Raymond of Toulouse, Godefrey of Bouillon, Baldwin of Boulogne, Robert of Normandy, Stephen of Blois—usually the younger sons of landowning families, each with a sizable private army and with distinctly secular ambitions. The Armenians, too, were a decidedly rough lot. Consider the story of Thoros and Baldwin. Thoros was an Armenian, a tough old feudal baron who at the age of sixty had driven the Turks from the city of Edessa. From far-off Constantinople, the Emperor Alexius Comnenus (doubtless short of the wherewithal for more tangible rewards) had bestowed on Thoros the title of Curopalates—Guardian of the Palace. Soon afterward, Baldwin of Boulogne arrived in the neighborhood with a private army, while around the same time a large Turkish force was threatening to move back against Edessa. Thoros suggested that he and Baldwin should make an alliance, but Baldwin demurred. Finally, Thoros offered to name Baldwin co-regent of Edessa and officially adopt him as a son. This strange adoption ceremony took place in

Thoros's palace one afternoon in 1098. According to one account, Baldwin and Thoros first stripped to the waist. Then a "doubly wide shirt" was placed over both of them, and the two men "rubbed their bare breasts against each other." Later, the same procedure under the shirt was repeated between Baldwin and Thoros's wife, "the elderly Princess Sophia." As with much of the rapport between Armenians and Crusaders, even the magic of that loony rite didn't last very long or create any very inspired friendship. The Turks were temporarily detoured from Edessa. But Thoros soon found himself on the wrong side of a palace intrigue and was "dragged from his chambers and torn to pieces by the crowd." Baldwin, who had remained tactfully neutral while the townspeople hacked up his lately acquired foster father, then proclaimed himself Count of Edessa.

Still, by the arrival, a hundred years later, of the Third Crusade—the one involving Richard Cœur de Lion and the Kurdish general Yūsuf ibn-Ayyūb, otherwise known as Salāh-al-Dīn, or Saladin—the Armenians were very much a presence in the Levant. For example, Prince Levon of Armenia was one of six noble lords in attendance at Cœur de Lion's marriage to Princess Berengaria, on Cyprus. And eight years later, when Prince Levon arranged to have himself crowned King of Armenia, it was no longer to Constantinople—his nominal source of patronage—that he looked for official approval but to the nearby, boisterous colonists from Western Europe. The coronation occurred one day in 1199, in the mountain fortress of Sis, the Armenian capital.

The Chancellor of Germany arrived from Saxony, representing the German emperor, who had just died, and brought with him a fine gold crown. The Archbishop of Mainz appeared, representing the Pope and bringing a jeweled scepter. From Constantinople, the Byzantine emperor—not to be left out—sent down another crown. Cœur de Lion himself was back in England, but he dispatched a present of a jeweled silver casket, lately stolen from a Sicilian monastery. Eight ambassadors from the Caliph of Baghdad attended, as did a retinue of eight hundred Crusader knights from Antioch, who "performed feats of jousting and brave horsemanship." Thus: King Levon of Armenia.

I thought, This was a bizarre corner of history. "Listen." I read to my wife: "At King Levon's court, Latin and French were spoken as well as Armenian," and: "He modeled his court on Frankish models, introducing many French titles for offices . . . for instance, bailiff, mareschal, seneschal, and so forth. . . . The High Court was established at the royal capital of Sis, modeled on the Assizes of Antioch. . . . There were also special courts under the jurisdiction of the Latin knightly orders such as the Hospitalers."

She laughed. "But it sounds sad," she said.

"How was it sad?" I asked. "Because the Armenians copied the French? Because it didn't last very long?"

"I don't know," she said. "Maybe because of what I hear in your voice. I mean, part of you claims to be this rational observer, and yet another part of you still seems to be trying to justify Armenians in Western terms—you know, that history we were all taught. Battles, generals, Crusades, Richard and Saladin and Robin Hood."

"That's not it at all," I said.

"All right," she said. "But why do you care so much that they seem European?"

One morning, Sarkis and we, and also Vartan, visited a refrigerator factory. It was a scheduled visit, impossible to get out of. Earlier, Vartan had announced over the telephone, "I understand you wish to see an electronics factory." What I had had in mind was computers. I had thought it would be interesting to look at an Armenian computer operation. "It has been arranged," said Vartan.

We went out to the factory. It was a large Victorian structure: bricks and steel girders and a glass roof—a bit like a nineteenth-century railroad station. Inside it were refrigerators. They dangled overhead from a conveyor cable, hundreds of white boxes swaying, moving slowly through the great room. Men in work clothes and women in scientific white coats reached up and did little things to the appliances as they passed by.

We were introduced to the plant manager, a short, fat Armenian with glasses and a harried smile. My wife asked him questions about "production volume" and "units per hour," which did not surprise him but which surprised me. Later, we were introduced to the Worker of the Month, a stout, red-faced old fellow with many gold teeth and enormous hands.

We stood in a room full of huge, silent machinery and had tea with the plant manager and the Worker of the Month. The Worker said that his son had just been accepted by the University of Erevan. He was a physics student. It was a very sweet moment. Even the plant manager seemed genuinely happy for him and clasped the old man about the shoulders. One knew that this was a model factory, but surely this could not have been a model event. I thought for a second of when I was a boy and heard the bartender at the Golden Horn announce that his son had been accepted into the Curtis Institute. Aspirations everywhere!

Afterward, outside the factory, as we were walking abreast down the sun-drenched street, Vartan said to Sarkis, "We hope to get our refrigerator next year."

Sarkis said, "We had ours last year. But we are still waiting for the telephone."

"I have the telephone," said Vartan.

"What do you think of Vartan?" my wife asked me.

"I don't know," I said. "He seems nice enough, but I can't guess what he's thinking. He seems very efficient—a young man on the way up in the Committee. I don't think he gets on too well with Sarkis."

"Sarkis is an émigré," she said.

"What do you mean?"

"Vartan was born here. Sarkis belongs to one of the

Armenian families that moved here right after the war. I think maybe that makes him more excessive."

"How did you know that?" I asked.

"He told me," she said.

"I find him hard to be with," I said.

"I know that," she said. "He feels it, too. He thinks you're finding it difficult to be here."

"That's not so," I said. It made me furious to be patronized by Sarkis.

"Well, sometimes you still act as if Armenians had nothing to do with you," she said.

ONE EVENING after dinner, we walked with Sarkis in a small park that had a pond with ducks on it and fountains splashing.

"How safe it feels here!" my wife said.

"Of course it is safe," said Sarkis. "We Armenians are a peaceful people."

We sat on benches opposite each other in the twilight. In the distance one could hear music playing—a popular tune on a loudspeaker. Some teen-aged boys walked by. They stopped at the pond, reached in their arms—shirts and all—and rubbed water over their faces, and went off laughing.

"In America, I hear, the youth are very violent," said Sarkis. "Here we have no such problem. Armenian children respect their parents."

"That must be nice for parents," my wife said.

"I know that your children are not violent," said Sarkis. "Armenian blood does not incline to violence."

For no reason, I asked, "Where were you in the war?"

"In Egypt," Sarkis said. "I was in the Armenian colony in Cairo and worked for the British. I was a clerk. They didn't treat me too badly, either, but after the war, when they had no more need of us, they went back to their old habits."

"And you came here?"

"I came here. It was the most fortunate thing I have ever done. I have returned to the Armenian homeland, and I am a citizen of the Soviet Union." He looked at me. "And you— were you in the war?"

"I was too young," I said. "I was at school."

"That was also fortunate," said Sarkis. "Armenians have no use for wars."

THAT NIGHT, I had some wretched dreams. Although the dreams (for there were several, blurring into one another) were about war and battles, in the center of each dream was a kind of dread—not so much a dread of war, or even death, as a somehow deeper dread of being *lost*. Although from whom or what was never clear. In one dream, I was alone in an unknown country. It seemed an endless dream, whose scenario was filled with ruined buildings, vast silences, train rides in empty carriages—at one point, a wooded avenue, quite pretty, with tall trees and fallen leaves, and lined with silent, empty tanks. In another dream, I seemed more actively to be searching for someone—my wife and children, as I imagined. There was a huge white hotel, bathed in sunshine, with orange trees in the garden and with the interior crowded with soldiers, mostly pilots. My wife and children were by a swimming pool. But my search persisted. I didn't know for what. The anxiety was quite excruciating—a feeling of being somehow kept away, or kept apart. I woke up shivering, hazily recalling the dream images of search: an area of rubble, wreckage—perhaps a city—which led suddenly to a field, an endless field of tall yellow flowers.

I looked at my wife asleep beside me. I thought (the thought coming from I knew not where), Sarkis and I are both in some way lying to ourselves.

Some time went by. The days were very hot. Each morning, the sun was higher above the olive hills, and warmer—a distant, glaring white circle that hovered over the unfinished pink buildings, the trees, the statues, the jangle of the traffic.

We went to visit old churches out in the dry countryside. There was a place called Garni, on the edge of a cliff, with dark pine forests all around and the racing water of a silvery river far below. Great slabs of black stone overgrown by weeds. Broken pieces of columns lay strewn about, decorated by Armenian stonecutters of long ago with designs of pomegranates and geometric shapes. It was a ghostly place, shrouded with trees.

There was also Zvartnots. I would say the name over and over to myself: "Zvartnots. Zvartnots." It sounded somehow so Armenian: a sound not like any other. Here were the remains of a great church, now lying in ruins on the plain of Ararat. We were almost familiar with Ararat by now, accustomed to looking over our shoulder at the sky and seeing the mountain's blue mass, the rim of snow. If Garni had been dark and hidden, Zvartnots was full of sunlight and stood blithely exposed upon the plain. Wild poppies grew amid the ruins, and one could see places where the invading Arabs had once built crude, cobbled fortifications around the sculptured columns. I thought, Darkness and light, perhaps the Armenian ambivalence.

IN THE STEAMY AFTERNOONS, I continued to read Armenian history. It required persistence on my part, for many times I found it hard to understand what I was doing in Armenia, and felt discouraged, not knowing what it was I expected. My wife seemed happy, although we fought sometimes. At any rate, she liked to see new things and to observe the exotic landscape.

For example, I read about King Hetum I of Armenia, who in the thirteenth century had journeyed for seven months and four thousand miles to pay a call on the Mongol chieftain Mangu Khan, in Karakorum, the great tent city of the Mongols. Armenian historians seemed eager to note that this was the first official visit by a Western ruler to the leader of the Golden Horde. Another "first"! Apparently, Mangu —who was Genghis Khan's grandson—received King Hetum "with courtesy and high honor," and even agreed to a rather short-lived mutual defense pact against the Muslim Mamelukes of Egypt.

It was history, I knew, but it sounded dreamlike. It made one wonder: What had the Great Khan and the Armenian king talked about? Had Mangu played dumb, like Sitting Bull, puffing on his pipe while fearsome Mongols put on a casual display of flaying prisoners or shooting arrows while standing on their heads and riding backward? Had Hetum rustled about the tent city (not yet visited by Marco Polo) in royal silks, politely tasting Mongol yogurt, talking to himself alternately in French, Latin, and Armenian? Did either of them have any idea in which direction history was headed?

It was surely not headed benignly toward the Armenians. Up in the northern tier of Asia Minor, as the Byzantine empire had shrunk steadily back to Constantinople, the Armenian plateau—so-called Greater Armenia—had become literally overrun by waves of nomads from Central Asia: Turks, Mongols, and the Tatar followers of Timour Lenk, or Tamerlane.

Down by the Mediterranean, in Cilician Armenia (where Hetum ruled), the situation was not much better. Muslim warriors had recaptured for Islam most of the Crusader principalities, with the result that Christianity had virtually disappeared from the Levant, save for the islands of Rhodes and Cyprus, and for the small kingdom of Armenia. This lesser Armenia was reduced to a few mountain fortresses: a defensive Christian enclave within a sea of Islam, which now reached to the gates of Constantinople.

The Armenians, one could see, had made two crucial bets. A long time back, they had bet on Christianity. More recently, they had bet on the Crusaders and the growing power of Europe. These bets were not in themselves wrong, for the dynamics of Christianity and Europe were such that both forces would sweep over much of the world. But it seemed that the Armenians had been in the wrong part of the world to make these bets—or, at any rate, to hope to collect on them.

AN ARMENIAN CHRONICLER, who remained behind on the Armenian plateau, described the first wave of Tatar nomads as follows:

Now, however, we shall also tell what these first Tatars resembled, for the first who came to the upper country were not like men. They were terrible to look at and indescribable, with large heads like a buffalo's, narrow eyes like a fledgling's, a snub nose like a cat's, projecting snouts like a dog's, narrow loins like an ant's, short legs like a hog's, and by nature with no beards at all. . . . Their broad faces were plastered with a poisonous mixture of gum. . . . They killed without mercy men and women, priests and monks, making slaves, taking the deacons as their slaves, and plundering the churches of the Christians without fear.

THEN, there was the story of the last king of Armenia. His name was King Levon V, and, by the time he reached the throne, Greater Armenia had been totally overrun by the Turks, and Cilician Armenia was little more than the city of

Sis. Even this outpost didn't last. In 1375, within a few months of his coronation, Levon and his subjects were besieged by an army of thirty thousand Mamelukes, half of them mustered by the governor of Aleppo. What the governor of Aleppo wanted with Sis was never clear. Perhaps it was "strategic." Perhaps he just knew he could take it. Finally, King Levon surrendered Sis, and thus the Kingdom of Armenia, and thus himself. The inhabitants were not totally slaughtered; some were permitted to become converts to Islam, and some escaped north to Constantinople, which was soon to have its own troubles. The Kingdom of Armenia, however, disappeared within the Mameluke empire —until that, in turn, was supplanted by the Ottoman Turks.

As for Levon himself, his was an odd and wistful story: true and bittersweet and unreal in the manner of chivalric fable, or perhaps in the manner of much of Armenian history. After the surrender of Sis, he was taken as a prisoner to Cairo, where he remained for seven years in a royal prison, perfecting his calligraphy and writing petitions for his release. Eventually, some European in-laws (the kings of Aragon and Castile) provided a ransom, and Levon sailed from Alexandria to Rhodes, and thence to Europe.

In France, ex-King Levon was received by King Charles VI, who gave him a house and a pension and invited him for dinner. The two men apparently became friends. The Armenian king taught the French king to play chess, and they often played in the evening. They also talked often about France's endless and ruinous war with England, which had been going on for decades, and came to be called the Hundred Years' War. Levon kept urging Charles to get out of the war—thereby, one imagines, freeing his army for one last, great Crusade to liberate Armenia from Islam. Charles invariably replied that peace with England was a fine idea, but that a cease-fire was an impractical step for him to undertake unilaterally.

In the end, Levon himself went to England, and there is a text of the speech that he delivered before King Richard II and Parliament, where *"nostre cousyne le Roi d'Armenie"* proposed an end to the Hundred Years' War—a proposal that was briefly considered and then abandoned. Levon stayed a while longer in England, perhaps peering at the dense dark woods and cold marshes and huge, coarse blond people, and then went back to Paris, where he died. King Charles provided an appropriate funeral for him, and he lies today in the basilica of St. Denis among the kings of France—in some ways as logical a resting place as any other for the last king of Armenia.

I said to Sarkis one evening at dinner, "I hadn't realized that the Armenians were so European."

"We're not European," said Sarkis. "We're Indo-European. That's not the same thing."

"I know," I said. "But there must have been a kinship between the two races—at least, at the time of the Crusades."

"Do you know something?" said Sarkis. "There should have been a kinship, but there was not. For one thing, Armenia was so far away. For another, don't you know, we were the rug merchants, the traders." As he said it, he laughed. "I remember that when I was a boy in Cairo they used to tease me about selling rugs. They did not mean it badly. It was a joke. But still I sometimes got sick of it." He looked at me. "It is something we Armenians have to get accustomed to, do we not?"

I felt a sudden rage within myself at these seemingly casual remarks, and, in fact, could hardly speak. I could see Sarkis's face staring at me, his plump hands on the table; he was wearing a gray, thickly knotted necktie. What had he said? "We were the rug merchants, the traders."

Afterward, my wife said to me, "Did anyone tease you at school about being a rug merchant?"

"No," I said. "Or I can hardly remember anything like that." But it wasn't true.

NONE OF IT was true, I realized. Not so much whether I had ever been teased for being a "rug merchant" as what I really felt about it. A great rush of memories overwhelmed me: small anecdotes from the past; trivial, unimportant remarks or jokes—many of them so petty I was ashamed to recall them. And not always from long ago: just before we embarked on this voyage, I remembered, an old friend of mine, wishing us well, said, with a laugh, "Now, don't get taken by any of those wily Armenians."

Wily Armenians! Rug merchants! Traders! What in hell did those things matter, I thought, trying to be more rational about it. But something had been let loose inside me—a shame, an anger. And I knew suddenly how it mattered. It mattered because it was supposed to matter. It mattered because I had said that it couldn't, mustn't matter. It mattered because my father had said that none of it existed.

We were walking with Sarkis through a museum, a museum of Armenian art objects: ancient pots and urns, crude wooden chariots and spears. I could hardly see any of the exhibits, let alone think about them or listen to Sarkis's incessant commentary, for I was still consumed by rage. I remember staring dumbly at an enormous orange-colored wine jar, peering at it studiously, and thinking, My secret is that I have always hated being an Armenian. I haven't ignored it or been shy about it—I have hated it. Because I was given the values of the Europeans and *they* despised the Armenians. And I have hated my father not, as I have thought all these years, for being too strong a figure or too authoritarian but because he, so to speak, stepped back and gave me to the Europeans.

What was that refrain I so recoiled from? "My father had committed no crime . . . my poor father . . . my father . . ."

And then, as if the rage had burst, I thought, Ah, fathers! How hard it is to be a father. And I thought of mine: his cool, elegant, impassive face, the face that sometimes smiled in public but rarely in private; the sad eyes; the English manner; his care that I become English, American—anything but Armenian.

We had moved on past the orange-colored urn and were standing in front of an ancient chariot. "A war chariot of the middle Urartian period," Sarkis was saying.

I said, "When did the Armenians stop being warriors?"

"What do you mean?" he asked.

"I mean, when did they stop being warriors and start being traders or rug merchants?"

Sarkis laughed. "Ah, rug merchants!" he repeated. He didn't know whether I was joking or not, and I didn't, either. "If you are serious," he said, "I think the answer is that there was no one time when they started to become traders. But the period you were just reading about, when the Armenians migrated from the mountains to Cilicia—

that was when they gave up their historic pursuits and turned to trade."

"What about the horses?" I asked.

"The Armenians were historically great horsemen," said Sarkis.

"What about the soldiers and the commanders of cavalry?"

"Yes, Armenians were great soldiers," said Sarkis.

I realized that he didn't understand me, and that in reality I was asking questions of myself, or perhaps of my own fantasies.

My wife and I sat out alone on a kind of restaurant terrace. It was early evening, the sky still light. People were lined up opposite for a movie.

I said, "All along, I've been trying to prove something, and it's not provable."

"But who said you have to prove anything?" she said.

That seemed sensible, although it was a hard idea to accept. I thought, People don't know anything about Armenians. Even Armenians don't seem to know about Armenians.

The next day, we were parading around yet another fine old Armenian church, out in one of the valleys, about an hour's drive from the city. It was a tranquil place: an ancient stone structure set against the dark trees and alpine meadows—a structure of dark-brownish stone slabs, smooth and weathered by age, which was quite small but very compact and stocky (like the Armenians), with a conical roof over the center, covered by tiles.

It was pleasant to be up near the mountains, where there were wild flowers and the grass looked less dry. Sarkis, in his ever-present brown suit, tightly buttoned, clambered over parapets and gravestones discoursing on Armenian architecture. It seemed that he especially favored the Austrian art critic and historian Joseph Strzygowski, who in 1918 had formulated the theory that key elements of both Byzantine and Western European religious architecture derived from the Armenians. "You know, Strzygowski has said that the Greeks with Saint Sophia and the Italians with Saint Peter's only elaborated on ideas that the Armenians first developed," said Sarkis. "Is that not something, my friends? Is that not a proud claim for Armenian architecture?" Sarkis bent down and picked a wild poppy from near a gravestone and handed it to my wife. I considered for a second whether Sarkis might not in some way be fancying her, but it didn't seem likely.

"What made Strzygowski think that?" I asked.

"It is very simple," said Sarkis. "It is a matter of the dome's being placed over the *square*. The Romans, as we know, placed their domes over circles, over circular structures. But the great architectural achievements of the medieval period and of the Renaissance came from the dome's being placed over the square. Strzygowski said that this form evolved first from the ancient wooden houses of Central Asia and was then perfected by Armenian architects as early as the fourth century." Sarkis sat down on a low wall, partly in the shade, and mopped his forehead with a handkerchief.

"Can we see some of those fourth-century churches?" my wife asked.

"Alas, that is a problem," said Sarkis. "They do not exist any longer."

"Did they exist in Strzygowski's time?" I asked.

"Alas, no. That was Strzygowski's problem, too. None of our early domed churches were still standing when he wrote his thesis." Sarkis got to his feet, pulling his jacket tightly about him, although the day was warm and becoming warmer. "It could have happened, you know," he said. "It is a plausible theory. But I admit that it remains controversial." He suddenly waved his arms, a stout figure in the middle of a graveyard, waving his arms at the passing clouds. "Look at the flowers!" he said. "Are they not beautiful? This lovely old church! Is it not beautiful here?"

ON OUR WAY BACK to town, we stopped to have lunch beside the road—sandwiches out of paper bags. There were some scrawny cattle in the distance. Fields on either side of us. Two trucks of laborers passed by—men of all ages, with dark eyes and mustaches, and holding long-handled hoes. I was aware of something's having happened yesterday, but I wasn't sure what it was, or how to talk about it. Before going to sleep the night before, I had been conscious of having admitted something shameful, having admitted some deep and shaming secret in simply acknowledging my revulsion (my shame) at this disparaged side of the Armenian character—the rug dealer, the wily merchant, the Levantine trader. But somehow today I didn't think I felt ashamed.

I asked Sarkis, "What was it like when you worked for the English?"

"It wasn't so bad," he said. "I had had a good schooling. I was the assistant to the head of a large warehouse. A military warehouse." He smiled. "That was when I had my motorcycle. 'Motorbike,' they called it."

"I meant, what was it really like?"

"What do you mean?" said Sarkis.

"I mean, what was it like to be an Armenian?" I said.

We were sitting on a rough stone fence. Sarkis had an

orange in his hand, which he was peeling with a penknife. He peeled it slowly, with a practiced hand—the orange-and-white skin unwinding in a steady ribbon.

"It was difficult," he said. "It was a very difficult time. It is hard to explain. You see, I had much ambition then. I was a young man. I was not bad-looking, either. I always liked the English."

"What did they think of you?" I asked.

"Oh, I was Sarkis, Sarkis the Armenian. But, you see, they were kind to me. When I was eighteen, I was chief assistant to this man, Mr. Peterson. He said he thought of me as a son."

"Where did you live?" I asked.

"I lived with my family, naturally. Where else should I live? We had a small house—part of a house, with another family. We lived in the Christian quarter. It was not far from the English."

"What went wrong?" I asked.

"What do you mean, what went wrong?" said Sarkis.

Sometimes he exasperated me. "I mean that you left Cairo, and this fine English employer, and you came to Soviet Armenia in 1948, when it couldn't have been much fun here."

"In 1947," said Sarkis. "No, it was not what you call fun." Then, "I don't know why you ask me these things."

"Because I want to know about you," I said. It was true.

"I'm not sure I can tell you," said Sarkis. "You ask me why I left Cairo. There were two reasons. The stinking poverty there had forced me toward the Communist teachings. And I was Armenian. I wished to return to my homeland."

"And what else?" I asked.

"There was nothing else," said Sarkis. The uneaten orange rested on the stones beside him. His eyes seemed to roam across the empty fields. "There was one thing," he said. "I fell in love with this girl, an English girl. She was going to the college. I would meet her after working. She was not very pretty, but I liked her very much. It is all so long ago that it is hard to remember. She had very long hair, and sometimes she used to ride behind me on the motorbike. We never really had plans to marry."

"But you were both in love?"

"Yes, but I was ambitious. Mr. Peterson had said he might take me into the business."

"Didn't he help you with the girl?"

Sarkis laughed. "No. You see, she was his daughter. He said that I had betrayed him. Oh, it was a terrible time. For a while, he wouldn't speak to me. The girl was sent away. You know, I don't remember her very well any more. Long hair and skinny legs—too skinny, I always thought. But I remember Mr. Peterson and Mrs. Peterson. One afternoon, I went to their house. I had been there before, of course, because I was his chief assistant and had taken messages, but I had not been there many times. She was very upset. Mr. Peterson kept saying, 'Don't get so upset, my dear,' but she got upset anyway. She kept calling me 'Jew' and sometimes 'Armenian' and sometimes both—'Armenian

Jew.' It's funny—I have often heard the English use that expression, although I think it is impossible. Catholic Protestant!"

"And so you left?"

"Yes, naturally. I had no choice. At first, I went to work for a rival company. I had this plan that I would rise high up in the rival company—control it, maybe—and then drive Mr. Peterson's company out of business. I had dreams that I would someday drive up to the English club in my motorcar and my girl would see me—how well I looked, how prosperous—and would know what she had missed. Oh, I had many youthful, vengeful dreams. In the end, I was ashamed of my desire for vengeance. My brothers wanted us all to move here, and so I did."

The afternoon was silent—silence everywhere. A large bird, perhaps a hawk, floated over fields far away. Sarkis slowly ate his orange. Then we walked down the dirt path to our car, which stood baking in the sun. Pausing beside the car for a moment, Sarkis said, "You know, about all I can really remember of that time is the day when Mr. Peterson said he thought of me as a son."

LATER THAT NIGHT, I thought, I am a son, and how can a son turn against his father? How dreadful it is! But then what strange creatures are fathers: these household Abrahams, with their knives raised on high—knives that take on all manner of shapes and forms, that descend in all manner of arcs. I thought, My father never raised his knife over me. I am no Isaac, and he was no Abraham.

I fell into sleep, half sleeping, thinking of how we were all together once, some long ago—a place of green fields, a picnic place. I remembered our dog had been there. My father wandered off. I could see him, a slim figure standing silhouetted beside a tree. Then, somehow, there were soldiers, and black shapes of airplanes overhead. We were in a prison above a rushing river—dark rocks below. I thought I saw Sarkis somewhere. I thought, If only Sarkis and my father can somehow meet, they will arrive at a plan—or at least an understanding. But my father was nowhere to be seen. Men with helmets roamed the hills. My wife was shaking me. "It's all right," she said. And, again, "It's all right."

After a while, I got out of bed and walked over to the chair by the window. It was quite late. The lights of Erevan were low. The square was dark. Everything seemed still. I watched a distant red dot blinking in the sky—a far-off plane—and remembered the figure standing silhouetted beside the tree, and thought, I love him anyway.

It had been agreed that around ten in the morning my wife and I should go with Sarkis to the Institute of Ancient Manuscripts: the Matenadaran. But by the appointed time, and even thirty minutes after the appointed time, Sarkis had not shown up, so for a while we milled aimlessly around the steps in front of the hotel—an area, scantily shaded by two or three frail trees, where, as always, a certain proportion of the male population appeared to spend part of its morning, leaning against the wall or standing in little conversational groups beneath the low branches.

My wife seemed irritated with me anyway. I wasn't sure exactly why. I thought, Perhaps because I woke her up with my nightmare. Then I thought, Perhaps because I embarrassed Sarkis in getting him to tell us his story. I asked her if that was it. Naturally, she said no. A bit later—we were still pacing about in front of the hotel—she said, "Well, of course. When someone like Sarkis puts his chips on the Soviet Union, on Soviet Armenia, it's the bet of his life. You can't just *talk* about it. I mean, it's not a matter of easy choices—like does one prefer Coke or Pepsi."

"I didn't think we were talking about that," I said.

"I know. You thought you were talking about Egypt.

Egypt and his English girl. But you kept raising these *questions.*"

"Is that bad?"

"I don't know," she said. "I've never been in his position. But I'm sure that's why he hasn't shown up."

"I'll go and call him," I said.

"He doesn't have a phone," she said.

We waited a little longer. There didn't seem anything else to do, and it was entertaining, in a way, to observe the drama—or, rather, the non-drama—of the shifting, leaning, standing, quietly talking groups of men. There seemed to be more tourists in the hotel, too. Two days ago, we had seen a handful of elderly French people—with a little tricolor provided by the management upon their table—seated primly in the noisy restaurant, surrounded by Armenians, but they had soon vanished as mysteriously as they had appeared. Now onto the steps emerged some German businessmen with dour faces, carrying briefcases and wearing raffish, double-knit suits. And then, unmistakably, there were some English. Evidently not businessmen but tourists. They stood there on the hot sidewalk in front of the hotel—oh, unmistakably English! First the voices. Then the *aspect* of the group, which numbered about a dozen. The men were middle-aged, save for one or two, and wore safari jackets, thick twill trousers, and sort of fly-fisherman hats. The women were of comparable age, surely wives, and were dressed in cardigans and tweed skirts. Some wore hiking boots, and there was a pile of camping gear behind them on the steps.

"Perhaps they're spies," my wife said. "Trying to blend into the surrounding countryside."

They seemed quite marvelous. Only yesterday, I realized, I had been cursing the English, sharing Sarkis's bitterness—in fact, extracting his bitterness to somehow accompany my own. And now here they were—an English touring group in Armenia. I decided to talk to one of them, and went over to an elderly fellow standing about, puffing at his pipe.

"Are you going to be here long?" I asked.

"In and out," he said. "We'll be in and out."

It turned out that they were members of a Yorkshire bird-watching club and were engaged in a spot of hiking and bird-watching around the Caucasus. "Last year, we went to some of the southern regions of America," he said. "By any chance, are you American or Canadian?"

"American," I said.

"Well, then you must know the Carolinas. Simply extraordinary shore birds. I knew we'd be in for a treat, but I had no idea of the actual *variety* of the specimens."

I asked him what he thought of Armenia.

"Oh, fascinating. A fascinating place. Yesterday, we were climbing that mountain—what is it? Not Ararat. The other one."

"Aragats," said a woman in a duck-shooting jacket, who had joined us.

"Yes, Aragats." I reminded myself that Aragats itself was more than thirteen thousand feet high. "About halfway up, some of our party—I regret I was not one of them—spotted *two* varieties of hawk that I must say none of us even knew existed in this part of the world."

"One variety," said the lady. "The other turned out to be a rough-legged hawk."

"Oh, yes. Well, it was a rough-legged hawk after all. Not so rare, but still rather unusual in my opinion."

"And how do you find the Armenians?" I asked.

"Which Armenians?" said the man. "Oh. The people?" He took a puff at his pipe. "Fascinating," he said. "Utterly fascinating."

"They're really quite charming," said the lady.

"Of course, I wouldn't *haggle* with any of them if I were you!" said the man, with a laugh.

My wife was tugging me by the arm. "Come on! Come on!" she said. "Vartan is waiting."

You bastards, I thought. "Those bastards!" I said to my wife. And "Why did you pull me away just then?"

"I don't know," she said. "I didn't think you were interested in birds. Besides, Vartan *is* waiting."

Vartan, our official guide, stood beside a car. In the last few days, he had apparently acquired a slight suntan. His hair was tousled, and he seemed hot—although he was coatless and tieless, for a change, which gave him an almost sporty look.

He said, "Sarkis is indisposed, and so he has asked me to accompany you."

We decided to go, as scheduled, to the Matenadaran. "I am not too familiar with the books," said Vartan, "but I will try to be helpful."

"I really just want to look inside it," I said.

It was a large and churchlike building set against the side of one of the hills. Within were a number of people, mostly schoolchildren on a tour—giggling young faces, the girls with great red bows in their hair, everyone being shushed by the teachers. The old manuscripts were locked away in glass cases. There were displays of tiny Bibles, no larger than a couple of thumbs, and of huge volumes in ancient, hand-worked leather.

"How meticulous and delicate the workmanship is," my wife said.

I thought, How meticulous and delicate and obsessive. I remembered those tiny carved boxes in the apartment of the old man on Thirty-third Street. His whole apartment had a kind of miniature, concentrated, hand-carved look—obsessive, and airless, too.

We looked for a while at the bright colors of the illuminated pages: the tiny, glowing figures in red, blue, and gold; the angular Armenian lettering of the Gospels. It was hard to know what it all meant. The manuscripts and old Bibles rested serenely under the glass. The schoolchildren giggled and poked one another. "Here," said Vartan, and he read dutifully from a display card, "This is part of the Bible from the Armenian church at Van, which was smuggled away by two sisters when they fled from the Turks. When one of the sisters died by the roadside, the other one retained the Bible and brought it here." The book in question was a considerable volume—perhaps two feet in length. There were dark stains across one of the pages. It was hard to know what any of it meant.

Vartan was clearly not in his favorite milieu, although he was trying to be polite. "Let's take a walk somewhere," I said. Outside, it was a changeable kind of day. Gray clouds were moving across the hills, and a cool wind blew.

"Perhaps you would like to see the new football stadium?" said Vartan. Clearly, Vartan wanted to see the new football stadium.

"All right," I said.

We left the car where it was, and walked for a long while down streets—streets with old buildings, streets with new buildings. Flower boxes hung from most of the windows. I said to Vartan, "Have you ever thought of yourself as a trader?"

He looked at me, smiling, uncertain. "What is that—a 'trader'?"

"A merchant," I said. "Somebody who makes deals."

"Who makes deals?" said Vartan. He laughed. "No. Why should I think that?"

We had come to the stadium. It was an enormous place, obviously very new: one of those molded-concrete structures, with a great bowl of seats rising up in a futuristic design, the oval of deep green far below.

"It is beautiful, don't you think?" said Vartan. He seemed much pleased.

"Yes, it certainly is," I said.

"I come to all the games," he said.

We wandered about the great gray concrete seats, solitary dwarf figures in an empty coliseum. Some bulldozers were still working on something down below.

"What did you mean about the 'trader'?" said Vartan. "I do not think I understand."

"I'm not sure myself," I said. "In other parts of the world, Armenians are often thought of that way—as traders. Buying, selling . . ."

"I have not heard," said Vartan. He pointed down toward the distant scoreboard, which had lettering on it in Russian as well as Armenian. "Our next game is with the Ukraine," he said. "At the present, our team is No. 2, but, of course, the Ukraine is very good."

It began to rain lightly, and we walked back in the drizzle. Gray water ran down the gutters, and the leaves on the trees looked fresh and almost glistened.

"I should have brought the car," said Vartan.

"No," I said.

We all knew it was nice this way.

Back in front of the Matenadaran, Vartan said, with a smile, "This buying and selling—I know. You mean 'businessmen.'"

"I suppose so," I said.

"Yes, we have *businessmen*," said Vartan, relieved at having cleared up the problem. "But I am not one of them."

We said goodbye at our hotel. "Did you like the football stadium?" said Vartan.

"Yes, very much," I said.

"It is a good stadium," he said. "We will win a lot."

Inside, Sarkis had left a note and a book.

The note, in thick, measured handwriting, said, "I am compelled to give a special lesson today. But I know that you will go to the Matenadaran with a guide from the Cultural Committee, and so you will not understand anything or learn anything. Therefore, you will do this for me. You will examine the book of colophons I enclose. For there are voices in this book, and you must try to hear them. Your friend and kinsman, Sarkis."

That evening, I took up the book that Sarkis had left—*Colophons of Armenian Manuscripts, 1301–1480*. It was in English, and handsomely designed, although at first glance it seemed an obdurate and unlikely thing to read. Colophons, after all, were short notes or messages "written, as a rule, by the scribes upon the conclusion of the production of a manuscript," according to their translator, Professor Avedis Sanjian. "Occasionally, they were written at the end of long sections of a text; there are also brief colophons which appear on the margins." My wife was sitting on the bed reading a book about the California Gold Rush. Outside in the square, there was the familiar sound of loudspeaker music. A casual crowd of people had gathered by the fountains—men and women idling in the warm summer's night. I began to read:

> VILLAGE OF SERKWILI: At this time there occurred a massacre of innocent Christians. . . . For, instigated by Satan, Djihānshah Mīrzā, of the Scythian race, assembled many legions of troops, besieged the citadel for four months, and caused them much anguish, for many died of grief.

MONASTERY OF SEWERAK: . . . The accursed dog [from the nation of] archers, Shāhrukh Mīrzā, arrived with numerous . . . troops. He devastated Armenia, carried off many into captivity and slaughtered them, he demolished and burned, and forced many to renounce their faith.

MONASTERY OF HERMON:
    . . . In bitter and grievous times,
When many in the land were persecuted,
Some dwelt among bushes,
Some fell prey to the wolves,
Many became victims of the famine,
Fathers disavowed their children.

VILLAGE OF SORI: . . . This holy Gospel was copied . . . in bitter and anxious times, during the khanate of Uzun Hasan, who in this year . . . shed much blood.

ALT'AMAR: . . . [This was copied] during the khanate of Iskandar Mīrzā of the nation of the archers, a Turk by race, who . . . caused ineffable and unrecountable bitterness throughout our land, and I cannot describe in writing the destruction of our country and the decimation of its population. For this is the tenth year that the tempest of God's wrath has visited our country on account of my multitudinous sins.

Page after page was filled with such notations. Brief jottings, as it were, from a bygone time: from the fourteenth and fifteenth centuries—that period, known to us in the

West as the Renaissance, when in the East the plains of Asia Minor and the Armenian plateau were at the mercy of various Turkish, Mongol, and Arab invaders.

At first, I found these colophons difficult to read, for there seemed to be no "story" to them, no order, no purpose. A list of messages from a remote time: disjointed messages, messages of woe and anger about unknown persecutors and nameless victims, about long-vanished, exotic-sounding tyrants. Djihānshah, Iskandar, Uzun Hasan, Bayandur Beg, Shāhrukh, Kara Yūsuf.

"And in this year there occurred a severe plague in our land. . . . And for two years he [Iskandar] ransacked and plundered our country. . . . We took to flight and wandered about in numerous places."

The sense of misery—for it was a litany of lamentations—appeared endless.

"It was a sight to behold the awesome moaning and lamenting over the dear ones, for the mother wept over her son, the sister over the brother, the bride over the bridegroom; and they received no consolation from any quarter, neither from God nor from man."

All the same, I kept reading, and I soon realized that I was strongly affected. Perhaps it was the mood of the evening—although, as I remember it, the only quiet was in our room, for the night's street noises continued for a long while unabated outside the open window, and at one point you could hear a dance band from the hotel's dining room playing nineteen-forties American foxtrots in a cheerful, stately measure. Perhaps, too, it was that something had changed between Sarkis and me, for he had asked me to try to *hear* something in these colophons. I believe "hear" was the key word, for what had at first seemed like dry words upon a page—a catalogue of dry words—now began to come through to me as voices.

I thought of the history I had read in the past few months, with its careful narrative of events and wavelike happenings. Battles. The death of kings. "At this time, there occurred a massacre. . . . In this year, there arrived locusts." I thought, too, of the ancient Armenia I had read about: the kings of Nairi; the sturdy mountaineers who clambered around the rocks above Xenophon's army; the horsemen and horse breeders; old Narses at the gates of Rome; even Thoros and his double-shirted ceremony. I had supposed that all that was real enough, and had clutched it as if it were some solid family tree, some solid *warrior* family tree that I might hold on to and be enhanced by. But surely *this* was real, too—these bitter and anxious times, these Hasans and dread Iskandars and poor, shame-ridden monks huddled in the cellars of their dark churches. More real, perhaps.

"This Holy Testament was begun and completed in bitter and anxious times when we were quivering at the hands of the infidels, for charity and mercy among men have disappeared."

"Sultan Mahmat . . . raised an intense storm upon the Christians and also upon his own people, by transplanting them from place to place, by imposing levies, and by causing other anguish."

Sultan Mahmat, I remembered, was the Sultan Muhammad II, who finally wrested Constantinople from the last, shadowy Byzantines; who transported eighty sea galleys overland to the Golden Horn; who employed the greatest cannon anyone had seen in the world; who was a leader of warriors, a collector of Greek books. The man who captured the One Great City, the city whose magic presence even the Turks Greekified—εἰς τήν πόλιν ("ees-teen-polin," or "to the city"), which five centuries later officially became Istanbul—and who instantly decreed its improvement, commanding the "importation of the skilled artisan populations of the Greeks and Armenians."

I thought, But what do I care about this Sultan Muhammad, with his fine cannon and his Greek books? What I care about are the people buried in the historian's sentence— the "skilled artisans," the Armenians.

By then, it was late at night. Over on the bed, my wife was long asleep. The lights in the square had gone out. The music had stopped. The summer crowd had vanished. A white moon had moved halfway across the sky.

As I read the colophons, I thought, They are like messages in bottles, messages from some long-ago sea wreck, messages written by men.

"They put the wondrous bishops to the sword; they ground the heads of the pious priests between stones; they cast the flock of Christ as food for the dogs. . . . Like the threshing-floor of flails, they thrashed the children with their horses; and, in place of grain, rivers of blood began to spring forth, and in place of straw the bones flowed forth like dust."

I thought, Perhaps strangest of all is now to be a modern man, an advanced citizen of an advanced country, and to scarcely conceive of the possibility of an unreceived message, a communication without a communicatee, a bottle that does not drift up to shore—some friendly shore somewhere.

The sky outside my window was clear, blinking with stars. But just then the darkness of the world seemed over-whelming, as did the sense of unheard voices.

A conversation with Sarkis.

I said, "I would like to know more about the Turks and the Armenians."

"The Turks are a despicable race," said Sarkis. "They massacred our people."

"Yes, I know that," I said. "But there must have been more to it."

"*More* to it!" exclaimed Sarkis. "What more can there have been? Murder is murder, is it not? Did you read the book of colophons I left for you?"

"Yes, and I was very moved by them," I said. "The Armenians seem to have suffered a great deal."

"You see, even *then* they were killing our people," said Sarkis. "For hundreds of years, we were persecuted by the Turks. What is it you want to know?"

"I want to know why."

"Because the Turks were savages," said Sarkis. "Have you not read what they did to us? To our women and children? Were these not the acts of savages?"

"But what did the Armenians do?" I asked.

Sarkis looked at me. "What do you mean—what did they do?"

"What did they do?"

"The Armenians did nothing," said Sarkis. "They were the slaughtered."

I thought, It keeps coming back to that. The Armenian refrain: "We were murdered. We were innocent. We were slaughtered. We did nothing." It was supposed to evoke compassion, I knew, and each time I willed the compassion forward, but it would not come. I felt a shame before Sarkis and myself. I also felt, There is something amiss with that refrain.

WHO were the Turks? I tried to read about them in books. For example, in *Turkey* (Geographical Handbook Series): "Chinese annals also record in A.D. 545 the rise of the Tukiu clan of the Hsiung-nu . . . who gathered other tribes and settled before 600 near the Caspian Sea, extending their rule thence to the Sea of Japan." And Professor David Bivar, in an anthology entitled *Central Asia:* "The expulsion of the Juan-juan dynasty from the Mongolian steppe was the result of the rise of the Turks, who thus make their first appearance in history. . . . The founder of the Turkish empire was the chief called in the Chinese sources Tu-men."

The Turks had been a huge association of nomad peoples, an amalgam of families and tribes, some strong, some weak, some primitive, some more advanced, most of them warrior-herdsmen shifting about on the ocean of the central Asian steppe, doubtless much like the North American Indians of long ago—sea creatures of the great land mass, drifting, grazing, hunting, fighting, propelled periodically by waves (of competition or of hunger) toward a distant shore, which in the case of the Turks was generally westward. Among the great nomad tribes were the Oghuz, the Uighur, the Kirgiz, the Pecheneg, the Kipchak, the Khazar. Even the names, at least in Anglicized form, had a somehow American Indian sound to them. The Oghuz in western Asia had been conquered by the Arabs and converted to Islam. At the beginning of the eleventh century, about the same time that the Byzantine Emperor Basil II was dismantling the native garrisons of the Armenian plateau, the Oghuz overthrew their Arab governors, and one of their more advanced and aggressive clans—that of the Seljuks—moved farther west, across the formerly Arab-dominated regions of Iran, and then north into Armenia and the Caucasus, and south to the Persian Gulf. From *Turkey:* "Though originally not very numerous, and wandering herdsmen rather than warriors, the Seljuks easily imposed their rule over the settled populations . . . while they adopted Arab and Persian cultures and combined them with Greek craftsmanship, as their fine buildings show. They left no literature; but their Ottoman successors owed much to their administrative experience."

"THE TURCOPHILES are always speaking about 'the glories of Turkish civilization,'" said Sarkis. "There has never been a 'Turkish civilization' to speak of."

"What about the Ottoman empire?" I asked.

"To begin with, the Ottomans were a minority among the Turks," said Sarkis. "By far the majority were the Turcomen—bandits and barbarians. But the Ottomans were cleverer than the majority. Do you know how they became so great? They persuaded the Turcomen to do the fighting for them. The *razzia,* they called it. The raid for plunder. The ignorant Turcomen did the fighting, and the Ottomans advanced their empire."

"Then the Ottomans were civilized?"

"They were civilized for Turks," Sarkis said.

THE TRIBE OF OSMAN, it was once called. The Arabs spoke the name as "Othman." The Byzantines transformed it again, to "Ottoman." The Ottoman Turks. By all accounts, they were one of history's great success stories. Back in the thirteenth century, Osman's tribe had been granted a small fiefdom in western Asia Minor by the dominant Seljuks. One hundred years later, the Ottomans controlled most of Asia Minor. Soon, they overran the Balkans. In 1453, Sultan Muhammad II captured Constantinople. His grandson Sultan Selim I defeated the Persians in the east, and took Syria and Egypt from the Mamelukes—in the process becoming the protector of the sacred cities of Mecca and Medina. Selim's successor, Sultan Suleiman I (the Magnificent), pushed farther into Europe, capturing Belgrade, defeating the Hungarians, and reaching the gates of Vienna.

By the end of the sixteenth century, the empire of the Ottomans was at its peak. The Ottoman Navy roamed from the Persian Gulf to Libyan Tripoli and Algiers. Ottoman beys governed territory that reached from the Armenian plateau across the extent of Asia Minor, Egypt, Libya, Greece, and the Balkans—an empire larger, even, than that of the Byzantines.

It was hard to consider this empire of the Ottomans without a certain astonishment. For it was so extensive, and powerful, and disorganized—and full of paradox.

I MADE some notes about the Turks:

From the start, the Ottoman state was autocratic, militarist, and religiously conservative. Temporal and spiritual leadership were combined in the person of the sultan, who was regarded as "the Shadow of God on Earth." Beneath him was the grand vizier, who managed the government—called "the Sublime Porte"—with the exception of the royal palace. In charge of religious matters was the sheikh-ul-Islam, who from the time of the magnificent Suleiman was head of the Ulema (Assembly of Learned Ones), and who did not manage the royal palace, either, although in some respects he was superior to the sultan, for only with the sheikh's final consent could a "holy war" be declared or the sultan himself be deposed.

The Janissaries: The name comes from the Turkish *"yeni cheri,"* which meant "new troops." As the wars in

Christian Europe ended, thus ending the supply of slaves, a policy of *devshirme* ("tribute children") was institutionalized. Young boys were taken from Christian parents, especially in the Balkans, and were farmed out to Muslim families in the provinces, converted to Islam, and then removed to Constantinople. The most physically fit were inducted into the Janissary Corps. They were trained rigorously in the arts of war, and lived apart from the regular army, in their own barracks. They were a dangerously independent elite body of troops. On initiation, they took a vow of celibacy and kept religious vigils. They prayed frequently, and doubtless furiously, and practiced "mortal combat" on one another, and in the heyday of the Ottoman empire they were the most feared—the cruelest and most efficient—body of troops in the world. By the sixteenth century, they were becoming decadent and more trouble than they were worth. Celibacy ended; free-born Muslims were admitted, many of these the sons of Janissaries; and the membership grew to an unwieldy peak of a hundred and thirty thousand. In keeping with the original savage monkishness of the order, their military titles were drawn from humble kitchen nomenclature. Thus, the senior commanders were Soup-Men. Other officers were Cook, Head Scullion, Water Carrier, and so forth. One of the traditionally dreaded moments of Ottoman political life was when the Janissaries overturned their giant soup kettles in the barracks square—symbolically indicating their displeasure with some recent action of the government's, and the likelihood of an imminent coup d'état. The corps came to an end when masses of Janissaries were cannonaded to death by a fed-up sultan in 1826—an event referred to in Turkish history books as "the Auspicious Incident."

The Harem: The word originally derived from the Arabic *"harām,"* which meant "that which is unlawful." For example, the area around Mecca and Medina was said to be *harām*—and so consequently the word came to signify "holy," "protected," "sacred," and, finally, "forbidden." The Ottomans did not invent the harem, for it had existed as far back as the empires of Assyria and Persia, but, as with many features that they borrowed from other cultures, they formalized and expanded it. The nominal head of the Ottoman harem was the sultan's mother, the *valide sultan*. Beneath this august personage stood the various mothers of the sultan's children. Beneath them were the favorite ladies, the novices, the female slaves, and also, as the enterprise grew, the royal princes, who received vague educational courses in Islamic doctrine and court protocol. The actual head of the harem was the chief eunuch, who after the sixteenth century was invariably black. He was known as the *kislar agha* and was a considerable figure in the royal harem—or, rather, in the seraglio, which was the name given to the entire palace complex of fourteen mosques, military school, ten kitchens, two bakeries, two hospitals, sports fields, arsenal, and harem. As a child, he had probably been sold into slavery by his parents somewhere in Africa; then he had been castrated en route to Constantinople at a desert stopping place along the

Nile, with everything removed by knife or sharp stone, and the patient permitted a few days to heal, buried in the sand. Now, with such traumas behind him but surely never completely out of mind—for it appeared that even total castration, if it took place after the onset of puberty, did not always remove sexual desire—the *kislar agha* was both a political and a military power in the capital. He had a small private army of his own, and three hundred horses for his personal use, and he also had his own jail and torture chamber. He maintained a steady level of income by his right of "inspecting" the funds of the imperial mosques. He alone might be the confidential messenger between the sultan and the grand vizier. He alone might approach the unapproachable sultan at any hour of the day or night.

It seems odd to think of the notions of masculinity and virility so often associated with this fussy and peculiar institution, which in fact contained the corrupt and neurotic *aghas,* the hundreds of aimless and unoccupied women, and the young princes, almost actively barred from any kind of serious education. To be sure, now and then there were some lighter moments. "It has been repeatedly affirmed," wrote N. M. Penzer in an excellent book, *The Harem,* "that when . . . favoured concubines enter the sultan's bedroom, which is not allowed until his Majesty has already retired, they approach the foot of the bed, lift up the coverlet, and raise it to their forehead and lips. They then creep in humbly at the foot of the bed, and gradually work their way upward until they are level with the sultan." Still, for both parties—the man in the bed as well as the girl crawling up it—it must have been the most confining of prisons.

The *Millets:* The Turks followed the Arabic pattern of dividing society into religious rather than national units. After the capture of Constantinople, each of the major *rayas* —or "flocks," as the non-Muslim populations were officially called by the Turks—were formed into separate religious entities known as *millets,* or "communities." Thus, all Greek Orthodox members of the empire were placed under the Greek patriarch, and all adherents of the Armenian Church were placed under the Armenian patriarch. In a sense, this office of patriarch was a considerable one, al- though—as with an ambassador from a foreign state—it was apart from the mainstream of official Turkish life. Even so, the Armenian patriarch, for example, ranked on a level with the higher Turkish pashas. He maintained a small police force of his own, and a private jail (although presumably not a torture chamber). Moreover, he was responsible not only for the spiritual life of his community but also for such matters as public education, civil administration, and the collection of taxes—the taxes due to his own administration as well as the "annual tribute" owed to the sultan.

This *laissez-aller* policy of the old Ottoman empire was a peculiar thing to observe. On the one hand, there was the autocratic sultan, and a rigid state belief in conservative Is- lam. On the other hand, there was the Armenian patriarch, with his own police force, collecting taxes. What did it mean? From *The Emergence of Modern Turkey,* by Bernard Lewis: "The Ottoman empire was tolerant of other religions, in accordance with Islamic law and tradition, and its Christian and Jewish subjects lived, on the whole, in peace and security. But they were strictly segregated from the Muslims. . . . Never were they able to mix freely in Muslim society. . . . If the convert was readily accepted and assimilated, the unconverted were extruded." One thing it seemed to mean was that the Armenians were second-class citizens.

I TRIED to discuss this matter with Sarkis—not to complain about the situation, Lord knows, although that is what I felt like doing, but because there were things about the position, or role, of the Armenians in the Ottoman empire that were not yet clear to me.

I said, "You know, in some of the books I've been reading the Armenians don't seem to have come off too well beside the Turks."

"Of course they didn't," said Sarkis impatiently. (We were sitting on a bench near the middle of Lenin Square.) "The Armenians were *conquered* by the Turks. The Turks conquered everybody in those days." He stared down at a spot between his shoes. "Savages!"

"I meant afterward. When the conquering had stopped."

Sarkis looked up. "The *conquering* never stopped. The Turks were the masters of Asia Minor, of Armenia, of the

Balkans. They had their governors everywhere; their militia—"

"Well, that's what I meant." I don't know why I wanted so to pursue the matter then, when I could see that it offended Sarkis. I think I felt that there was some clue to be found. "At least, from what I've read," I continued, "it seems to me that the Turks were very much the masters, and that the Armenians had only a very token independence."

"What did you expect?"

"I don't know," I said. "But it seems to me the Armenians were placed in a subservient position. They accepted subservience—"

"You are wrong!" said Sarkis, suddenly red in the face. "You are wrong! You have read very wrong! The Armenians were better than the Turks. The Turks knew nothing! All they cared about was making war, and soon they stopped even doing that. The Armenians were civilized. In this so-called Ottoman empire, it was the Armenians who knew about administration, who knew about business, who knew about architecture, and agriculture, and—" Sarkis paused. I had never seen him so angry or upset. He looked at me, his eyes quite hard. "You come here to Armenia and all you care about are the Turks," he said. "What is it you want?"

"Maybe you won't understand this," I said, "but I want to know everything about the Armenians, and that seems to include knowing something about the Turks."

"I know what you want," said Sarkis. "You want to tear down your father."

"It has nothing to do with my father," I said, feeling angry myself.

"Of course it has," said Sarkis. "Fatherland, father. It is the same thing."

"My father is dead," I said. It seemed an insane argument. "Besides, I love him. I've always loved him." I knew that the last was not true, but I hated Sarkis then.

"Is your father dead?" asked Sarkis sarcastically. Then, "I could tell this from the start, when I first saw you. All that Anglo-Saxon coolness and detachment. Yes, that detachment! Not like a proper son!" I looked at him. He seemed to be shaking—his thick, compact body rocking forward at the waist. I wanted to say to him, "How dare you?" or some such thing. But then he turned his head away. "Your father was an Armenian," he said, in a voice that seemed quite hoarse. "You must respect him!" And then Sarkis suddenly took my hands in his, and I looked into his face and saw that he was crying.

After Sarkis had left—for he claimed a meeting or appointment at his school late in the afternoon, and soon departed by bicycle down one of the side streets, pedaling in a slow and stately fashion, his brown-jacketed back vanishing in the traffic—I wandered off on my own across the square, past throngs of men and women on their way back from work, past small children playing tag beside the fountains, past a gathering of Armenian policemen in Russian uniforms standing solemnly around a broken green motorcycle, past newspaper kiosks selling only *Pravda* and coffee shops selling only tea, and, not wishing to walk farther or to stop anywhere along the street, I made my way almost by chance into the museum.

Inside, it was quiet and nearly empty. Two elderly guards in rumpled uniforms sat at a card table near the entrance playing dominoes and drinking soft drinks. Behind them I glimpsed the hall with the war chariot and urns which Sarkis had led us through some days earlier. Downstairs, it was a museum of brittle artifacts and of domino playing. Upstairs, the wood floor of the exhibition rooms stretched out, gleaming and lately polished, beneath my feet.

Costumes and pieces of faded peasant dress hung on the walls.

What in hell had Sarkis meant, I wondered. I knew what he had meant about my "coolness and detachment," because I had heard that many times before—indeed, had heard it for much of my life, had come to know such a quality in myself, for apparently it was part of me, a segment of my nature, a character trait that friends could spot and discuss perceptively. *You're very analytical, you know. You have this detachment.* I knew that on a deeper level I wasn't detached or cool. I was anything but cool. But I also knew that I often seemed that way. It was a kind of curse, which I tried to escape from in my writing.

I padded through the hushed museum, alone in the empty halls, the floor shining like ice and having an air of inutility about it, like the floor of some aristocrat's ballroom. I attempted to keep my mind—or, anyway, my eyes—on the exhibits, with a view to educating myself and learning more about Armenia, not wasting the moment, and so forth. There were displays of metal bowls that had been made (or so a card declared) by Armenians in Persia. Some embroidered jackets from Armenians in Poland. Some wooden boxes from China. Armenians apparently were everywhere—blown like poppy seeds, sending back obscure handicrafts instead of postcards.

You must respect your father. The phrase ran through my head. It still made me angry that I should have been told this—by a stranger, by this Sarkis, this volunteer kinsman and friend! Did I not already respect my father? Did I not love him? To be sure, at times I experienced the reverse of such feelings—the child-rage of a forty-year-old son who had once felt threatened by his sire. But wasn't this common? And even these hard emotions were surely dwarfed by the compassion I had learned to feel for this man, who I knew had himself suffered greatly in his life, his fortunes, his career. If anything, I thought, I respected him too much.

By then, I had walked nearly to the end of the floor. I was about to turn around when, down a small corridor to the left, a solitary portrait suddenly caught my eye. Indeed, it did more than that—it gave me quite a jolt. At first, I thought it was a trick of lighting or perception. Then I thought it was a trick of the mind—my recent preoccupations having somehow jammed my optic nerve. There, at any rate, at the end of this narrow corridor (which led, as far as I could see, nowhere), hung a painting of a man in period costume. The background of the painting was dark and nondescript. The face of the man, however, was sharp and luminous, either from the gleam of the paint or from the museum lighting: my father's face.

As I came closer to it, my sense of normality returned, for clearly it was a painting of someone else, someone particular. The typewritten title card, taped to the wall, described him as a merchant of Erzurum, from the eighteenth century. But the face seemed uncannily like my father's.

I stared at the canvas closely, trying to see the markings of the artist's brush, the placing of the pigment, as if by observing it as an object, as paint on canvas, a man-fashioned likeness, I might separate the two presences.

It was a simple portrait, really—on the whole, pleasingly and conventionally done. The merchant wore a hat of dark-blue velvet and a ruffled white silk shirt. A gold chain hung from his neck. The look of the dress was *soigné* and European. The face itself was small-featured and intelligent, with a not large but definite nose, a thin mouth, and quiet, glowing eyes. The expression of the face was composed. Over all, the appearance of the merchant was of a man assured, elegant, in control. But how remarkable was the quiet, almost withdrawn brightness of the eyes!

I thought of my father, and, as I so often did when summoning him back from death, from incorporeality, from inside my head, my dreams—whatever "memory" is— in my mind I saw his face (was it from a photograph, an actual scene, an imaginary moment?) looking wordlessly back at me. Not really looking at me—just *looking*, looking out from somewhere, from himself, the way he often did. "Impassive": that word always came to mind. Yes, composed, elegant, coolly assured. And then I saw the eyes again, for if there was a silence to his eyes, there was also a glow, a heat, the most noiseless of passions. The eyes seemed almost to burn out at me. Burning eyes in a frozen face! I thought suddenly, It wasn't coldness or coolness that I had felt in him. It was never coldness. It was— How might one put it? An absence of temperature. A redirection of temperature—inward. But whose face was it I was looking at—the face in my memory or the face on the canvas? Or both?

The merchant of Erzurum stared down from the pale-green wall. Erzurum: I knew it from my readings as a moderate-sized provincial capital on the western edge of the Armenian plateau. Once, it had been the site of a Roman garrison. In Byzantine times, it had become a major caravan stop and the center of a flourishing textile and carpet indus-try. Since then, it had been under various Turk and Mongol administrations culminating in its capture in the sixteenth century by the Ottomans. I wondered how our composed and elegant merchant had fared with the Turks. From the dignified presence in his portrait, he had done reasonably well. Clearly, he was a man of substance, one of the top businessmen of the town—doubtless a leader of the Armenian *millet*. Did he sometimes have dinner—or, anyway, take coffee—with the Turkish bey, and discuss the new tobacco taxes and the gossip of distant Constantinople? Did he send away for shirts? Did his wife read aloud to him in French? Did he mind it that he could never have a serious place in governing his country, or that his Turkish neighbors sometimes called his son *"giaour"*—"infidel"? Or did he set his expression, freeze part of himself, his face—all save the eyes, which no man can control—and tap his finger on the coffee cup, and nod, and curl and uncurl his hand inside his well-cut pocket . . . and *manage?*

For an instant, I tried to imagine my father in the merchant's blue velvet hat. At first, I thought of it as a game, a conceit, but then my imaginings began to seem all too apt, even obvious. The obviousness of the image took my breath away. A merchant! Why not, I thought. The remote, vivid, controlled expression looked back at me from the dark canvas. I thought of Sarkis, standing on the stone wall in the graveyard, talking, gesticulating, waving hands and arms, profuse, volatile, excessive. So far removed from control and impassivity. And it came to me then and there that, all along, the two sets of mannerisms had been a variant of a single response—this cool, "un-Armenian" control and the shrill, "Armenian" excitability. They were twin symptoms, one bursting wildly outward, the other absorbed coldly inward. The merchant, my father, Sarkis—and how many others?—were the same.

I realized at that moment that to be an Armenian, to have lived as an Armenian, was to have become something crazy. Not "crazy" in the colloquial sense of quirky or charmingly eccentric ("My crazy old man!"), or even of certifiably mad. But crazy: crazed, that deep thing—deep where the deep-sea souls of human beings twist and turn.

It was near twilight. The sound of an old man coughing in a distant room sounded like falling china. I could not bear to stay in the museum any longer, and went down the stairs, past the empty card table, out into the soft and choky dusk, walking quickly across the square, as if on important business, and back to the hotel.

Up in our room, my wife had recently returned from

buying fruit and bread at the market. The hotel radio was playing Russian folk songs—the sounds of static and a balalaika. It was a tranquil domestic scene.

"Sarkis phoned," she said. "He was concerned that he'd offended you. What's been going on?"

"Nothing much," I said. "We were talking about Turks. Turkish civilization."

"You'd think that two Armenians could talk together about that without fighting," she said. She had a pile of strawberries beside the sink and was washing them. She seemed in a happy mood, and tapped her foot to the scratchy music. "A while ago, you didn't seem to want to get involved with Turks and Armenians," she said. "'All that massacre business,' you called it."

"I never called it that."

"Oh, you did. But what do you suppose changed?"

"I don't know," I said. "Maybe it's not a very easy subject to jump into."

"I guess it isn't," she said. "But I'm curious. What bothers you most about it?"

"You know, I don't think I'm really bothered," I said.

"Is it that the Turks were such bastards? Does it remind you of the Germans and the Jews?"

"All that," I said. "And the fact that the Armenians were so helpless."

She sat at the wooden table, plucking the green sprigs off the strawberries and putting the berries in a bowl. "How do you know they were?" she said.

"Because everyone says so."

She looked at me. "Maybe," she said. "But I don't believe it." And then, "You know, I wish just once in this whole damn time you'd *admit* to being really bothered!"

I thought of the frozen man in the blue velvet hat. Perhaps I, too, was the man in the blue velvet hat. And how could I explain to anyone about that?

We went on an expedition to Byurakan. Very touristic and semi-official: five of us packed into the ancient, run-down limousine, which was driven, fortunately, not by Sarkis, who—along with Vartan—sat in the front, generally silent, with a straw hat on his head, but by a tall, elongated teacher of mathematics named Arak, a "professional colleague" from the school, who smoked cigarettes incessantly and evidently enjoyed himself rushing through the yellowing countryside.

Byurakan—it was a little village, about an hour's career from Erevan, and also the site of a great observatory. The little village possessed such charm as similar places everywhere possess—which is to say, largely in the eye of the beholder. Tiny plots of dry soil with a goat, perhaps; some frantic chickens; one or two fruit trees bearing little bulbs of orange. The houses were of stone, and many of them contained new window frames but no windowpanes.

"Look," said Arak, puffing wreaths of smoke. "They will not have windows by Christmas. In my mother's village, it required two years."

"Christmas is six months away," said Sarkis, as if imparting official information. "They have things speeded up this year."

"Ah, yes," said Arak. "I can see."

A cluster of old women—or, anyway, of women who looked old—stood near the road, some twenty or thirty feet into the field, leaning on their hoes. Arak waved a smoky hand. One of the women waved back—surely the wave of a younger sister. I thought of a passage in Osip Mandelstam's *Journey to Armenia,* written during the dreadful nineteen-thirties, when the great and persecuted Russian poet was briefly "vacationed" to Armenia. It was about a visit to Byurakan, and it went like this (as translated by Clarence Brown):

Everywhere there were peasant women with tearful faces, shuffling movements, red eyelids, and cracked lips. They had an ugly way of walking, as if they had the dropsy or had strained a tendon. They moved like hills of weary rags, stirring up the dust with their hems.

The flies eat the children, gathering in clusters at the corners of their eyes.

The smile of an elderly Armenian peasant woman is inexplicably beautiful—there is so much nobility, exhausted dignity, and a sort of solemn, married charm in it.

I liked the part about the "exhausted dignity" and "solemn, married charm," and wondered if it was true—although perhaps, as with van Gogh's pictures of country life, it was enough that the artist had seen whatever he had seen.

Mandelstam had not mentioned the great observatory, and so probably it had not yet been built. Or maybe they would not show it to him, fearing that the Jewish poet might spot some altogether marvelous Jewish star out in the cosmos and publish the news abroad in literary quarterlies. Or maybe Mandelstam had been uninterested in observatories.

In midmorning, we trooped about like schoolchildren through the scientific facilities. There is this to be said about observatories in general: they are inevitably disappointing, because of their lack of frightening equipment and size, and because when photographers take pictures of giant telescopes they usually try to please by making the telescopes appear far larger than they are, and so when you finally see a giant telescope up close, you think, So what? Although, not being a child, you do not say it but instead mutter, "Ah, very interesting." There was this to be said about the observatory at Byurakan in particular: it was certainly disappointing in the traditional way, but there was also something appealing in its lack of pretension. There were no intimations either of importance or of the lack of it. Everything looked as if it needed paint, although when you examined things closely this was not always so. Here were some filing cabinets, there some telescopic equipment, also several old chairs, a table, an urn of coffee, a studious young man who disappeared, two amiable women, and on the outside there were flowers everywhere.

One of the amiable women showed us photographs of whitish spirals, some of which were very poetic and familiar. The roof was made to open by a push button, much like a garage door, and revealed a wedge of pale-blue sky. As it happened, the chief of the observatory, Distinguished Scientist Ambartsumian, was not in residence. He was in Houston, Texas, delivering a lecture. And why not?

Thus, instead of being able to interrupt the Distinguished Scientist and drive him mad with witless questions, we sat on the green grass outside amid the beautiful flowers and had lemonade in paper cups. Behind us rose a dome of the observatory. There was an air of calm, and even laziness, around us. We were in the presence of science.

I felt sad for a moment, sitting on the rough grass and thinking one of those banal travelers' thoughts: that soon we would be leaving Armenia, and—

And what? And would never tour the observatory at Byurakan again? It was not a thought that one pursued relentlessly.

"It's too bad you didn't get a chance to see Professor Ambartsumian," said Sarkis, in his hortatory manner. "He is a great Armenian scientist. There are many eminent Armenian scientists." And so forth. After a while, Sarkis wiped his brow, took off his hat, and lay back upon several flowers.

We were on the top of a hill, looking down on a valley filled with green and haze, and it seemed that one might be able to see far away, into other places and countries.

I asked Vartan, who had been silent for most of the trip, if he had ever traveled outside Armenia.

"I have been to Moscow," he said. "It was noisy, with many huge buildings."

"Have you been outside the Soviet Union?" my wife asked.

"No," he said shyly, as if harboring a secret thought. Then, "My wife wishes to go to California and see Mickey Mouse."

"Mickey Mouse!" said Sarkis.

"The amusement park," said Vartan.

"Amusement parks?" said Sarkis. "What foolishness! Listen to the dreams of these young people!" He sat up on the grass, blinking in the sun. "There is only one place to go, my friends. That is Paris."

"Ah, you and your Paris!" said Arak.

"It is truly the City of Light," said Sarkis. "Not even Leningrad can compare. Paris has everything—culture, beauty, beautiful gardens, exceptional food. I was there once, do you know?"

"He was there for two days," said Arak.

"Three days," said Sarkis. "What does it matter? I was at an educational congress—a congress of philologists. Many noted experts. We were in a tiny hotel, squeezed into rooms. They took us around in buses. But I was in heaven, every minute of it. I felt my soul purified."

"By the French women?" asked Arak.

"I was talking about my soul," said Sarkis. "The soul is the important thing."

"My wife would also like to see the Beatles," Vartan said.

"You know, I was inside the Louvre," Sarkis said. "All my life—in Egypt, here—I have heard about the Louvre. On the last day of our congress, I left our lecture—I was with Szabo, the Hungarian—and we raced to the Louvre. We looked at the Winged Victory of Samothrace. Such a beautiful thing, although it was surrounded by Japanese. I said to Szabo, 'Can you imagine that we are inside the Louvre?' He was very happy, too. Then we had to leave right away, or we would have been missed. But I am going to go back one day and see the Venus de Milo."

"You will never go back," said Arak. "One rapture is enough."

"I have already applied," said Sarkis. "There is a linguistic congress in two years."

"In Paris?" said Arak.

"In Helsinki," said Sarkis. "It's not the same thing, but it's almost the same."

A matronly woman from the observatory appeared carrying two handfuls of paper-wrapped sandwiches, which she placed gently on the ground one by one, as if they were turtles, and then she beamed and ambled away. We opened our sandwiches in the warm sun. I thought of the poor poet Mandelstam wandering about Armenia in the nineteen-thirties. Across the valley, far away from us, there stretched another range of mountains, dim and gold. I wondered if Turkey was beyond those mountains.

"What was it like here in the thirties?" I asked Arak, knowing that it was an impossible question.

Arak sat cross-legged on the grass, the sun glinting on his wide forehead. "It wasn't like this," he said. He started to eat his sandwich.

"How was it not?" I asked.

Arak looked at me as though to say, "If you have to ask the question, there is no way I can properly tell you." His face seemed very angular—chipped out of fine, hard wood and covered with pale skin. He put the sandwich in his lap and said, "There was no food." He said it flatly, almost in an amused manner, as if recalling a certain feature of the landscape. "I remember other things, of course, because I was a child. But what I remember most is that there was no food."

"In those days, there were many problems with agriculture," said Vartan, in his guide's voice.

"Yes," said Arak. "I think there were many problems with agriculture. What do you think, Sarkis?"

Sarkis was silent; shook his head. "I don't know," he said.

Arak said, "You know, we lived in Alash, a small village about forty kilometers from Nakhichevan. My father was a schoolteacher. Later, he was killed in the war somewhere in east Poland. It was a poor village—turnips, radishes, and rocks. Some time past, I think there had been cattle—or, anyway, people used to speak of it. 'We must get some cows or move,' my father would say, but, of course, we never did."

"Your mother is still in Alash?" asked Vartan.

"She was buried there," said Arak. "She was seventy-two." He stretched out his long legs. "One whole winter, she made us soup from grass. Grass soup! It was terrible. My mother didn't tell us at first. 'It is spinach soup,' she said. But, of course, there was no spinach. Then we saw her with the grass. My sister used to cry all the time, because she was hungry. Sometimes I think of that now and want to beat her with a stick, although she herself is now a grown woman with grandchildren. Imagine—a child who is always crying and you have no food to give it!"

"I have heard such stories," said Vartan, "but from earlier times."

"What do I know of stories?" said Arak. "But I will tell you about my mother's aunt. She was married to Melikian—old Melikian, they called him—and lived in the mountains. The village they lived in is no longer even there. Every springtime, we used to make the journey up into the mountains to visit them—the old people. The old man kept some bees, and he would make us presents of sticky combs of honey. Well, one winter it was very bad. It was the winter of the grass soup. Even in our valley we had almost no turnips left. And the snow was everywhere. The world was buried in snow! Nothing stirred. We tried to catch rats, you know, but even the rats had gone. My mother worried about the old people up in the mountains, because we heard reports from other villages of how bad it was. I can tell you that they did not tell the children much about it, but children always find out, do they not? And so one day—in March, I think, long before spring—we set out for the mountain village. It was right after a snowfall, I remember. We carried sacks of bread and also turnips. We could hardly find the village because of the snow, and when we got there the first person we saw was a woman huddled in shawls on a doorstep, crying in the cold. I think my father knew her, and he gave her some of the bread we had brought, and she took the bread and was eating it and crying."

"What about your mother's people?" asked Vartan.

"The old people," said Arak. "Yes. We came to their house. My father could tell right away. 'See, there is no smoke,' he said from the road. They must have been dead nearly a week—perhaps more. It was a good thing, too, that it had been so cold, for they were frozen solid. And their feet were bare. I said, 'Father, why were they not wearing shoes?'—because I had never seen the old people's feet like that, naked. And my father cuffed me with his hand, so that I nearly fell down. 'Enough of your questions!' I think he said. Have you ever eaten shoe leather, Vartan?" Arak asked.

"I never have," said Vartan.

"Me either," said Arak. "At least, I don't think so." He laughed and stood up, still holding his sandwich. He looked at it and began to eat. "Not bad," he said. "Our scientists have good mayonnaise."

It seemed to be much later than it was. There were a few white clouds in the sky. Far down in the valley, some cattle stood beside a grove of trees—black and brown shapes. Two slender birds, like swallows, turned in the cool wind.

"Let us be off," said Sarkis, hands in the pockets of his brown jacket. We trooped to the car, in single file, along the gravel path that led down from the observatory.

On our way back through Byurakan, we saw some schoolchildren standing by the side of the road throwing pebbles at a dry stream. "Do they still have many flies here?" I asked, thinking of the children in Mandelstam's journal.

"There are no flies here any more," said Arak as the yellow fields sped by.

As I thought about it later, there was something about Arak's coolness on the subject of those early hardships that took my breath away. For it wasn't necessary to have digested each word of *The Gulag Archipelago* to realize that death by starvation had been only one of the forms of horror visited upon the length and breadth of Russia during the Stalin years. (What estimate had Solzhenitsyn made—that one out of four citizens of Leningrad had been sent to prison or to a labor camp? One out of four!) Yes, one knew that death in the snowy silences of Armenia had been but one of the terrible acts that men had been required to contend with in those days, and that Arak's refusal to discuss the rest, to describe the whole of the iceberg—while somehow implying its presence—had been a stroke at once of bravery and of a frightening realism.

Beyond that, something else remained and worked in my mind as a result of Arak's story about the old people in the village. It was this: If Arak had been speaking the truth about the hunger and starvation of those times (and why should he not have been?), and if Solzhenitsyn had been writing the truth about the prisons and labor camps (and why should he not have been?), then how unbelievably terrible it must have been to exist anywhere in Russia—certainly in Soviet Armenia—during the long Stalinist nightmare of the nineteen-thirties and forties! Yet—and this was what I now noted—here was Arak, and here were how many others of his generation, and older, whom one saw every day on the street, overheard in cafés, observed standing upright on the buses returning from work, upright and proud. That was it! Not only had they survived the terrors and persecution but now they were on their feet, well on their feet: building soccer stadiums, pink stone apartment houses, statues, refrigerators, computers; fashioning fine, tall children; and talking of the past without that coloring of lamentation and self-pity which so many Armenians elsewhere seemed to employ when they talked about the Turks. For it seemed that even those who had not been personally involved, such as Sarkis, carried with them an "experience" of those earlier massacres—perhaps some racial memory of the events—like a poison.

I decided then and there to set down as directly as I could my understanding of what had actually happened between the Armenians and the Turks—in other words, to confront some of the things that I had read and thought about and kept myself detached from—and to see if some sort of meaning or coherence might not eventually emerge. Somehow, whatever had happened to the Armenians seemed to have been more than murder. But what, one wondered, could have been *more* than murder?

THE KEY to the puzzle lay, surely, in the nineteenth century, for it was toward the end of the nineteenth century that the so-called Armenian Question achieved a kind of international prominence, and that the proverbial roof started to fall in upon the Armenians in Turkey. It was strange to have studied nineteenth-century history so often in my youth but never with regard to Armenia. To be sure, Armenia did not occupy a large place in many history books. The Turks, for example, generally ignored the subject, dismissing the Armenians as one among "many Asia Minor peoples" who for obscure reasons had betrayed the Turkish trust and created trouble. The Europeans, principally the English (who, after the English custom, journeyed to remote places and turned out obtuse, carefully phrased journals), took much the same line, with a few notable exceptions, such as Arnold Toynbee, and with the added angle that any misfortune that had befallen the Armenians had doubtless been the result of their low—and, presumably, un-English—instincts for "trade." The greater part of Armenian history books were in their way no more helpful than the Turkish accounts, or non-accounts. If the Turks ignored the subject, the Armenians usually overwrote it. That is, the Turks were innately murderous; the Turks were savages.

Much of the story of the Armenians in nineteenth-century Turkey seemed to be closely connected to the person and personality of the thirty-fourth Ottoman sultan, Abdul-

Hamid II. When Abdul-Hamid succeeded to the sultanate in 1876 (as a result of his older brother Murad's having succumbed to a "nervous disorder" after three months in office), he looked out upon a still large but disorganized and declining empire of roughly thirty-five million people, of whom around thirteen million were Christian subjects of the Ottoman provinces of the Balkans, and around two million were Armenians, also Christian—some of them in Constantinople, some in Europe, a few in Syria, most of them spread out across Anatolia and the classic Armenian plateau, which had been divided into the six *vilayets* of Turkish Armenia.

For years, the Balkan Christians had been in revolt—inspired by the example of the French Revolution, incited by the liberal movements in Europe, at times assisted by the autocratic, imperial-minded czars of Russia. Lord Byron had died for "Greek freedom" at Missolonghi in 1824, five years before Greece gained its independence. (Not the least remarkable act of Byron's life was that he had spent the winter of 1816–17 in a Venetian monastery learning Armenian.) The Russian czars spoke solemnly about "protecting" the Balkan Christians. The majority of the Ottoman empire's Christians might be restive; the Armenians were not. The Turks regarded the Armenians as the *millet sadika*—the "loyal community."

In May of 1844, while on a state visit to Queen Victoria, Czar Nicholas I had observed to Lords Aberdeen and Palmerston: "Turkey is a dying man. We can try to keep him alive, but he will—and he must—die. I am afraid of no one except France. With so many tons of gunpowder close to the fire, how can we prevent the sparks from catching?" Thus, Turkey became known as the Sick Man of Europe, although its possessions were mainly outside Europe and although, as it happened, the word and concept of "Turkey" were still alien to the Turks. The French "Turquie" and the English "Turkey" derived from Medieval Latin: "Turchia" or "Turquia." However, the Turks thought of themselves as subjects of the Ottoman empire; "Turk" was a vaguely pejorative term applied to the peasantry. When, finally, in 1923, the Turks officially adopted the name, they transposed it from the European usage—"Türkiye."

By the time of Abdul-Hamid's accession to the throne—or, rather, to the sword of Osman—the "sickness" had grown worse. In part, this resulted from continued troubles in the empire's European provinces. More directly, it resulted from the magnitude of the Ottoman debt and the weakness of the Ottoman financial structure. Stated simply, European industry and capital were in the saddle. The Ottoman ruling caste, classic conservatives—still prisoners of a fading racial memory of war and plunder—had established neither; they had little to sell the world, and everything to buy. In the course of one twenty-five-year period, the rate of the Ottoman piaster relative to the pound sterling fell three hundred per cent. And when, in 1840, the government created a national bank, it fell hopelessly in debt within a few years, as it doubled and redoubled its borrowing—at the same time reducing its interest payments—so that the European central banks, which had gladly contributed to the sickness, were compelled to take a more active role in Turkish affairs in order to protect their investments.

Abdul-Hamid could do little about his European provinces' demands for independence except to try, with increasing trouble and bad publicity, to repress the demands, and, in the main, to watch with anger and impotence as the provinces broke away. He could do little about the financial mess—or, rather, *would* do little in the way of cutting down official expenses—and so was forced to accede to growing European control over the Ottoman treasury. In fact, for a while representatives of European banks administered the Ottoman debt from a special European office in Constantinople, placing liens against portions of Ottoman tax receipts in order to pay off their loans.

Impotence: an absence of potence. What little actual power Abdul-Hamid retained, he kept close to his vest and dealt out sparingly. He was an autocrat who liked surprises. For instance, soon after he became sultan the European powers and Russia held one of their conferences—in Constantinople, of all places—on what might be done about Turkey's disaffected European provinces and on the general question of Turkish reform. No Turks were invited to any of the high-level discussions. Abdul-Hamid remained quietly in his palace, playing Offenbach on the piano and watching the pennants on Lord Salisbury's yacht. One morning in the early days of the conference, while the delegates were seated at table drawing up their agenda, the guns of the Topkapi fortress commenced firing a salute. One hundred and one rounds. When the cannonading had stopped, the delegates were informed that the Sultan had just announced a constitution, which would make their presence no longer necessary. After the conference had broken up, Abdul-Hamid consigned the constitution to the limbo it had come from, and sent the Minister who had drawn it up for him into exile—and then had him murdered.

In many ways, Abdul-Hamid was an unusual man. Thirty-fourth Sultan of the House of Osman, Caliph of Islam, Shadow of God on Earth, he was of moderate height and slender build, with a pale, gravely handsome face, dark, watchful eyes, and a normally quiet and withdrawn expression. He was afraid of the dark. Also, fearing assassination, he rarely slept in the same room two nights in a row. For the same reason, on his weekly appearances in public—riding in a carriage to the Hamidiyeh Mosque—he kept a small child on his knee. No decent assassin, he reasoned, would be likely to kill a child. Indeed, Abdul-Hamid's feelings about assassination were such that he would not permit the word (or any of its synonyms) to appear in print. "So the Turkish newspapers attributed the sudden and simultaneous deaths of the king and queen of Serbia in 1903 to indigestion," wrote Bernard Lewis. "In the same way, the Empress Elizabeth of Austria died of pneumonia, President Carnot of apoplexy, President McKinley of anthrax." Abdul-Hamid maintained an extensive collection of pistols and other hand weapons, which he ordered continually from Europe, and one of which he kept at his side at all times. He was a good but impulsive marksman. On different occasions, several gardeners and a footman were shot by the Sultan as a result of coming upon him unawares. Also, the Sultan was fond of animals, and kept a private zoo on the grounds of Yildiz Palace. At Yildiz, too, he caused to be built two private cafés, which were modeled on ordinary Constantinople cafés and were at all times staffed with waiters, and where now and then the Sultan would stop (always the only customer), order a coffee, and express polite surprise that it should arrive so quickly.

If ABDUL-HAMID felt impotent rage against the Europeans, who seemed to have a mortgage on his empire and were always trying to tell him what to do, his feelings toward the Armenians were more complex and, in the beginning, less visible. One of the least visible threads, perhaps, was this: Since birth, Abdul-Hamid had been dogged by the rumor that his own mother was Armenian. It was not impossible, considering that the Ottomans favored non-Turkic *shiksas* for the royal harem. Rumor had it that she was either Jewish or Armenian. Her name comes down to us as Pirimujgan, which, at any rate, doesn't sound Jewish. No official announcement of Abdul-Hamid's birth was made until harem records were checked and rechecked. Finally, after an unprecedented three-day delay, the new heir to the throne was acknowledged, but a cloud hung over the event. Piri-mujgan herself died of consumption shortly afterward, and Abdul-Hamid was said to have always thought fondly of her. But all his life his attitude toward Armenians remained markedly private and intense.

Who were the Armenians—this "loyal community"—in those days? Much has been made in novels and histories written by Europeans of the Armenian merchant and trader —the thorn in the side of the more manly and hardworking Turk. Thus, recently an English writer, Joan Haslip, noted in a biography of Abdul-Hamid, *The Sultan:* "Owing to the aversion of the average Turk to any form of commerce, most of the business of the empire was in the hands of either Greeks, Jews, or Armenians. . . . [Abdul-Hamid's] interest in every form of finance was so contrary to the tradition of the well-bred Turk as to revive the rumor of his mother's Armenian origin." Miss Haslip doesn't explicitly criticize the Armenians (or the Greeks or the Jews) for engaging in trade, but the implication seems fairly clear: The Turks were a jolly lot, perhaps not clever in certain ways, but good fellows, full of breeding—probably rode well, too. The Armenians were genetically mercenary and obviously *foreign*.

The truth of the matter seems to have been better and worse than that. In a majestically dry and scholarly book about Armenian communities in the Ottoman empire, written by the same Professor Sanjian who translated the colophons, there is this revealing passage: "In the Ottoman administrative system the high-ranking officials of the Porte and the provincial governors derived their income not from a government salary but from legal taxes and extortions levied on the population over which they had jurisdiction. Each official was dependent on a banker, usually Armenian, who furnished him with capital on interest for securing an appointment and for the surety required by the central government for the proper transmission of revenues to the imperial treasury." This implied a fascinating state of affairs. First, the Ottoman ruling caste, while expanding its bureaucracy in the modern manner, had retained its anachronistic traditional method of dealing with it—disdaining to pay its administrators salaries and instead letting them somehow make it up in the field, skimming taxes here, taking bribes there. Then, on top of that, the Ottoman state had required these officials to put up capital for their jobs, and to maintain them with additional deposits of capital (against tax receipts) throughout the year. Thus, since the warrior Turks (who had not been successfully at war for two hundred years) had neglected to develop either capital or a banking system, or even bankers, the result was that their growing civil service was virtually pushed by its own government into a debtor-creditor relationship with the Armenian merchants and bankers. What folly for the Turks to have ar-

ranged things so badly! What folly for the Armenians to
have let it happen!

ONE HAS, then, a picture of a developing Armenian
elite in Constantinople. The Turks needed the Armenians,
who understood the new worlds of capital and commerce.
Also, the Armenians, armed with a literacy taught by their
church schools, often spoke several languages. They were
needed as translators and interpreters—as connections with
the Western world. A relationship almost of dependency
existed between Turk and Armenian, but it was a unique
and dangerous sort of dependency. For the creditor Armenians were in the minority and were Christian, and the
needful Turks were in the majority and were Muslim.

The mutual unawareness of these Turks and Armenians
seems astonishing, albeit human. Still, the Constantinople
Armenians were only a minority of their own people. The
majority of the Armenians lived where they had always
lived—in villages and towns across Anatolia and the Armenian plateau, side by side with the Turks, with whom they
had shared their homeland for over four hundred years.

In a little book called *Travels in Armenia*, by the Hon-
ourable Robert Curzon, published in London in 1860, and
lent to me in New York by the writer Peter Sourian, I found
the following description of the building of a "country
house" in Turkish Armenia:

When a house is to be constructed, a space of ground is marked out, perhaps nearly an English acre, and then part of the whole is excavated to a depth of five feet. Eight or nine tree trunks are placed in two rows as columns, with the larger branches planted across the columns as roof-beams. The center of the house is the stable. In a richer house, there are two stables and the roof is a snow field. A fire of dung, called *tezek,* is continually smoldering. There is a divan covered with the most beautiful carpets and large wooden pegs for pistols, guns, cloaks, anything else. The chimney rises two feet or so above the ground, with a stone on top to keep lambs or children from falling in, for these habitations are constructed on the side of a gentle slope with no fences to keep people off the roof.

Toward the end of the book, Curzon tells the brief story of Artin, the *oda bashi:*

In the month of August of last year, a [Turkish] merchant named Mehmed brought his merchandise to the inn, where he slept. Two soldiers were asleep next to him. In the morning, his merchandise had vanished and he accused the two soldiers of stealing it, but they denied it and were let go.

As it happened, a woman had seen them burying the merchandise, and when these were ordered to be dug up and found incomplete, the soldiers said that the *oda bashi* —the inn-clerk—had stolen the other half. The *oda bashi* was an Armenian, Artin by name. When he denied the theft he was ordered to be tortured into the truth. A metal drinking cup was heated over a fire and placed over his head. Then a cord was tied around two pig's knuckle bones and this was tightened around his temples until his eyes nearly came out. His front teeth were extracted and pieces of cane placed under his nails.

Unfortunately, under Turkish law only two witnesses are required for a conviction, and no testimony is accepted from women, foreigners, or Christians. I heard about this poor wretch's story and took the matter to the Pasha. He said it was not true and I believed him for I had found him to be at other times a straightforward and honest man. My servant, however, had looked in through the jail window and seen Artin's pitiable condition. I said to the Pasha: "This man has been tortured because he is Armenian." The Pasha again denied it, but the next morning released Artin, who was about thirty-five years old and bore terrible scars.

A few days later I was writing at my desk, when I heard a most extraordinary shuffling and screeching, as if several cocks and hens were suffering from strangulation. Along the floor of my house advanced the most strange and incomprehensible procession of men and women, crawling on their hands and knees, each with a rooster in their hands! One woman grabbed hold of my foot and began kissing it. Being horribly alarmed, I kicked as well as I could and asked my servant to get rid of the unsightly group.

Later he informed me that they were the family of

Artin, the *oda bashi,* and although they were pained that
I did not accept their poultry, they expressed gratitude to
him that I had saved their kinsman. In truth, it is clear
that fashions change everywhere, and that Turkey, like
the United States of America, is no longer a land of laxity,
where every free and independent citizen has the right to
beat his own nigger, or where the Sultan could cut off
fourteen heads a day!

At first, I felt furious at this Englishman's story. Had he
become "horribly alarmed" that those poor wretches were
trying to kiss his feet? And, as for the right of independent
citizens to beat their own niggers, was he trying to say that
the Armenians were the niggers of nineteenth-century
Turkey? And was he right? That was a mind-stopping
thought. In a rage, I read the story of the *oda bashi* to my
wife. She said, "But what are 'niggers,' anyway, except
people whom the ruling majority never looks at?"

I said, "But the Armenians seemed so badly off. Houses
underground! Fires of dung!"

She said, "Surely their Turkish neighbors were as badly
off, or worse. Look, Artin at least had an education. He
could read and write. He was a clerk."

All the same, something seemed true and sad about the
story—sadder, even, than the spectacle of the inn clerk being
tortured. Indeed, the act of torture seemed but an outward
sign of a far worse disease. For the first time, I had a profound sense of the depressed condition of the Armenians.

"Depressed condition"—the phrase went through my mind. No, I thought, it had been worse than that: *depression*. Might not a people existing too long in an untenable position, a barely tenable position, a diminishing position, experience the same symptoms of clinical depression as an individual? Might not a *people* show signs of listlessness, a glazing of the eyes, a lack of motive, an inability to get out of bed in the morning and look for better work?

My wife was looking through the Haslip book on Abdul-Hamid. "Listen to this," she said. " 'Both Abdul-Hamid and his immediate predecessors had treated the Armenians with tolerance and justice.' " She closed the book. "Obviously, everybody has different standards of tolerance and justice," she said.

As THE NINETEENTH CENTURY wore on, Abdul-Hamid's troubles increased, and it happened that the Armenians did nothing to lessen them. For the winds of reform and European liberalism had reached even the *millet sadika,* the "loyal community." The first indication of a change in temper occurred during the Russo-Turkish War of 1877–78 —a war disastrous to the Turks—when the Russians, eager to hasten the Sick Man to his grave, invaded not only the Ottoman Balkan provinces but also, on the other side of the Black Sea, Turkish Armenia. Abdul-Hamid, furious and helpless, was compelled to ask "the English woman," as he always called Queen Victoria, to stop the Russian advance, and after a display of Her Majesty's warships in the Dardanelles the Russians halted, and grudgingly pulled back from both fronts, although they were allowed to keep the three Armenian districts of Kars, Ardahan, and Batum. Abdul-Hamid was enraged to learn that some of the Armenians had actually welcomed the Russians. It was soon after this that England, anxious to keep Russia out of eastern Turkey, where it was always threatening to "protect Christians," became interested in the so-called Armenian Question—and Abdul-Hamid's dormant paranoia toward the Armenians intensified.

Liberal England, under Gladstone, was eager to take up the new Armenian cause. Conservative England, under Disraeli, preferred to accommodate the Sultan and keep the Suez route free of hazard. On either side of the issue, the English appeared to be involved. But what was the Armenian cause? It was a fairly modest one, by European standards: equality and freedom of opportunity within the Ottoman empire. Unfortunately, the European liberals, who were far away and remained far away, never seemed to realize that the implicit basis of the Ottoman empire was inequality. The sons of Islam had to be first. Therefore, somebody must be second.

What is interesting about this whole period is the mildness, almost the naïveté, of these early reform movements, with their political and literary ties to Rousseau and Montesquieu.

Life, property, and honor are the candles
of our hearts. . . .
Your law informs the Sultan of his limits.

Thus went a Turkish political ode of the eighteen-fifties, which was considered dangerously radical. Inform the Sultan of his limits? *What* limits? Early Turkish and Armenian reform groups seem to have been very close, for many of the young Turkish and Armenian men had studied together in Paris and London, and shared a wishful admiration for European liberalism. The first Turkish group, which was established in 1865, called itself *Yeni Osmanlilar* (New Ottomans), or, alternatively, *Jeunes Turcs*. The Armenians, some years later, formed two parties, one called Hentchak (Bell) and the other called Dashnaktsutiun (Federation). Though both were founded by Russian rather than Turkish Armenians, they were actively concerned with the plight of Armenians in the Ottoman empire. The chief aim of the Turkish intellectuals in those days was to obtain a constitution and a more representative government, and better controls on the state treasury. The chief aim of the Dashnaks—the more effective (and less Marxist) of the two parties—was to obtain religious freedom and tax relief, and also the right to serve in the armed forces. Neither Turks nor Armenians then seriously entertained the thought of abolishing the sultanate. Nor did most Armenians, unlike the Balkan Christians, express any wish to break away from the Ottoman empire. The great majority of the Armenian reformers—tinged, like the Young Turks, with varying shades of constitutional Socialism—wanted mainly to work within the system.

Abdul-Hamid's response to these new winds was probably predictable. Reform groups and political parties of any description were declared illegal and de-facto "revolutionary." Intellectuals, both Turkish and Armenian, were arrested, sometimes exiled, sometimes murdered. The Sultan seemed to have a special anxiety about the "Armenian revolutionaries"—the several hundred activists, mostly students. He forbade the Armenian language to be taught or to be spoken in public, and ordered that no mention of Armenia or reference to anything Armenian be printed anywhere in the empire. Also, he created an irregular force of Kurdish tribesmen—fierce, primitive Muslims who for years had drifted across eastern Turkey in a state of feud with the settled Armenian communities, which they periodically ransacked. These detachments of newly uniformed Kurdish cavalry were called the Hamidiyeh, and were posted as garrisons near the major Armenian towns, whose Armenian inhabitants Abdul-Hamid ordered to give up any weapons they might possess. In the meantime, the Sultan's private surveillance network was expanded to around twenty thousand agents, who dutifully filed reports with their employer; these eventually filled several rooms of the palace, and were read each day on their arrival by the Shadow of God, who soon read little else.

Abdul-Hamid's massacre of the Armenians began in the summer of 1894, with the capture by a Turkish patrol of two members of Hentchak who were traversing the mountains in the Armenian district of Sassoun. Orders were immediately sent from Constantinople for Turkish troops, accompanied by a detachment of Hamidiyeh, to raid Sassoun, in order to uncover such additional "revolutionaries" as might be hiding there. As it happened, the district of Sassoun was a natural fortress—a collection of villages perched high in the rocky mountains and inhabited by hardy and independent-minded mountaineers. The year before, they had refused to pay their taxes, complaining that the Kurds had already exacted tribute from them. They had demanded that the Porte control the Kurdish chiefs. Abdul-Hamid had responded by sending in troops, who, after encountering unexpectedly heavy opposition from the Armenians, ended by killing nine hundred of them.

Now the people of Sassoun again resisted the advance of the Turkish troops, and again they resisted effectively. For two weeks, the Sultan's soldiers and the cavalry that bore his name were held at bay on the craggy mountainside beneath Sassoun—and some were killed by the Armenians. Abdul-

Hamid, keeping himself more closely than ever within Yildiz Palace, reading his spies' reports, attending to the messages from his new telegraph, evidently believed that the moment he had feared and expected was now at hand: the Armenians within the Ottoman empire were in revolt. Down the same telegraph lines that had told him of the existence of the rebellion, word was sent to the beys of the eastern provinces to suppress the Armenian uprising before it could spread.

Far away from Constantinople, then, out of sight of the ambassadors of the European powers, a loosely organized process for the killing of Armenians spread across the towns and villages of Turkish Armenia. In some instances, an "official pretext" was found for massacre. For example, in the town of Bitlis a quarrel between an Armenian and a Turk over the price of two oxen resulted in the arrest and execution by Turkish police of a hundred and fifty Armenians as "revolutionaries" and the subsequent slaughter by an aroused Turkish mob of nearly two thousand. More usually, an Armenian was discovered—or merely suspected of—keeping a firearm or sword, whereupon a hundred or so of his neighbors might be rounded up and shot, as in Marash, or decapitated, as in Diyarbakir. In some places, hanging was preferred—Moush, for example, where twelve Armenian teachers from the local school were hanged, and left hanging. As time wore on, however, and there were no signs of interference from the ambassadors of tenderhearted Europe (who, to be fair, did not have their own telegraph lines to the eastern provinces), and no change of instructions from the Sultan, the matter of "official pretexts" came to be pursued ever more casually. That is to say, the idea of putting down a rebellion or of capturing dangerous revolutionaries seemed less and less to occupy the official mind. Instead, the procedure appeared to be generally like the following, which occurred in the town of Urfa.

There, one day, into the populous Armenian section rode the soldiers of the local Hamidiyeh regiment, which had been garrisoned some four or five miles out of town. Some Armenian shops were looted by these Hamidiyeh warriors. When a shop owner protested, his shop was set on fire. At one point, two Armenians tried with their fists and linked arms (since they had no weapons) to keep a group of the Hamidiyeh troops away from some Armenian girls. The two Armenians were seized and decapitated with cavalry swords. When other Armenians began to protest, the Hamidiyeh rode away, for they had done their job. And in an hour's time (some have said less) a mob of Turks approached the Armenian section. For two and a half days, this Turkish mob, soon joined by other Turks—all of them average Turkish citizens, ordinary co-inhabitants of the picturesque town of Urfa—roamed at will through the streets of the Armenian community. Most of the Turks carried clubs—thick hardwood implements that had the look (some said) of having been specially fashioned for the event—and not a few carried the *yataghan,* a kind of machete used in vine cultivation. Armenian men were killed wherever found. When some of the younger men attempted to fashion weapons with which to defend themselves, they were seized and killed in particularly horrible and degrading ways.

By the evening of the second day, many Armenians, especially women and their children (who had not been in any sense exempt from persecution), had taken refuge in their church, a moderate-sized and ancient edifice at the intersection of two streets. The Turks nailed broad wooden beams across the doors of the crowded church, so that they could not be opened from the inside, and then set fire to it. The blaze lasted all night long and into the morning, and, when it was over, it was estimated that around two thousand had perished inside—although some said later that the exact figure was closer to seventeen hundred but had been "rounded out," as is often done in matters pertaining to crowds and attendance. At any rate, none came out. Over all, in Urfa in those three days approximately ten thousand Armenians had been killed—a figure that has doubtless also been "rounded out" to some degree but that those who have studied Ottoman census and taxation records have in the main attested to.

This general procedure—of Hamidiyeh provocation followed by Armenian protest and culminating in rampage by Turkish mobs—was pursued, or by peculiar coincidence was adhered to, in most of the towns with large Armenian populations: Van, Bitlis, Erzurum, Diyarbakir, Marash, Trebizond as well as Urfa. After the Hamidiyeh troops had galloped away from the scene of looting and sudden violence, the Turkish mobs were never long in taking to the streets. Nor were the victims of these mobs always randomly selected; in numerous cases certain individuals, notably priests and schoolteachers, had clearly been singled out beforehand for special attention, of which death by hanging was not always the unkindest form.

IN A PERIOD of two years, about three hundred thousand Armenians were thus put to death within the confines of the Ottoman empire—and. in a peculiar kind of silence. There was a special quality to the silence that enfolded those "events." It was not the heavy historical silence that in times past had usually enveloped the murderer and his victim—the silence resulting from the remoteness of the deed and the ignorance of the listener, which had kept so many terrible actions hidden from the eyes and ears of the world. Think of the massacres of ancient history: tribes or armies caught in some unmapped valley far from home and slaughtered to a man, with no storybook messenger or herald to announce even the "facts" of the event. Think, for that matter, of the Armenian colophons: those despairing messages stuffed into the shipwreck bottles of history, actually buried in cellars— uncommunicated to anyone save God (who never answered), and scholars many hundreds of years later. "Like the threshing-floor of flails, they thrashed the children with their horses; and, in place of grain, rivers of blood began to spring forth, and in place of straw the bones flowed forth like dust."

What loneliness and silence surrounded these words when they were written! But consider: By the year 1894, the silence of the world had become less complete. For instance, a species of modern traveler had come into being, assisted by the railway and the steamship, tramping about the globe, busying himself here and there, observing this and that. In the fall of 1895, a group of German and Swiss schoolteachers were traveling through eastern Turkey. They passed a village where not a soul appeared to be alive. "A terrible plague," explained the guide. The schoolteachers saw blood on the walls of houses, and a village square where jackals and vultures still fed off the unburied dead. The advanced nations of the world had evolved postal services, and from this development came the "correspondent"—originally a simple letter writer in a distant place, eager to use the new system, to communicate. For instance, a Swiss schoolteacher traveling in eastern Turkey. Then, too, there was the telegraph—the "long wire"—still in its infancy. Like many infants, it was closely guarded by its parents—not its true parents, for those were the inventors, but, at any rate, its adopted parents, as perhaps one might call the proprietary governments. Consider the role of this new invention in the Turkish massacre of the Armenians. It was in many instances the telegraph that had transmitted the "information" about the Armenian unrest and "revolutionary societies." It was the telegraph that had then transmitted the "information" about the suppression of this "revolutionary activity." Finally, it was the telegraph that speedily and efficiently communicated to the world the Sultan's denials of wrongdoing. For, because of this partly broken silence of the new era of communication, some word, at least, had reached the outside world of the murderous happenings in eastern Turkey. Travelers had written letters, which were then published in European newspapers. Minor consular officials of the great powers, stationed in towns such as Erzurum and Trebizond, had communicated what they had seen or heard of the massacres—at least, as far as their embassies in Constantinople. In Europe, hundreds of miles away, spokesmen of the liberal movement (which had originally given voice to the Armenian Question) now expressed moral outrage at the reported excesses of Abdul-Hamid's Turks. In England, in 1896, former Prime Minister Gladstone, then eighty-six years old, emerged from retirement to make the last speech of his life, in Liverpool, where he inveighed for ninety minutes against the plight of the Armenians and characterized Sultan Abdul-Hamid as "the Great Assassin." In France, Georges Clemenceau proclaimed Abdul-Hamid *"le Monstre de Yildiz"* and *"le Sultan Rouge."* Even Queen Victoria wrote a letter: "Her Majesty would earnestly beg of the Sultan to enquire . . ." But the Sultan would have none of it. In a rare interview, granted to a representative of the London *Times,* he declared that the reports of Armenian massacres were "gross exaggerations." To the mild inquiries of the English and French Ambassadors, the Sultan's Ministers replied politely, or sometimes not so politely, that the situation of the Armenians was an "internal matter," and that, in any event, it had resulted from Armenian provocation. How many times in the course of the yet more murderous twentieth century would the world listen in to such verbal remonstrances and such official excuses and denials: "exaggeration," "provocation," "an internal matter." It almost seems as if with the arrival of communications it had in certain ways become easier to lie officially. Which is to say that a question-phrasing apparatus had been invented and developed, with its wires and transmitters and its appearance of communicating answers. But one man, or government, might still control the apparatus and the answers. And perhaps there was more to it than that. For previously the world had abounded in lies that no one heard. Now lies were heard all over the world, somehow dignified by their transmission through the apparatus, and even listened to with a kind of respect by the machine's new clients.

MEANWHILE, across the eastern provinces of Turkey—a Turkey whose political health was an object of such concern to European statesmen—the Turks continued killing and persecuting the Armenians. A letter from another Swiss teacher, who had been traveling in Anatolia, and whose correspondence was printed in a Zurich paper, read partly as follows:

In all the village of B—— I found not a sign of life.
The houses all stood empty and the doors of the small shops
were open as if waiting for customers who were never to
arrive. It was as if life had vanished from that section of
the world. Later, as we were on the road to K——, from
behind some rocks appeared six women, although so ema-
ciated and miserable it was hard to tell what they were.

They were Armenian women who had survived or
fled the massacre of their village by the Turks. We gave
them pieces of bread which they stuffed into their mouths
like wolves, or perhaps camp dogs. It was a pitiful sight.
They said that their menfolk had been slain or else had fled
north toward Russia, as one of them hopefully prayed.
They asked us if we would somehow get word to the men
that they might return, or get word to someone about what
had happened. We said we would do what we could, and
gave them more bread, and the poor wretches fled back
behind the rocks.

Get word to someone. The modern prayer. At around
the same time that the schoolteacher was writing to Zurich,
the French Ambassador in Constantinople, M. Paul Cambon,
was communicating as follows to Paris: "The [Turkish]
Government acknowledges that there has been widespread
unrest in the eastern provinces between the disaffected Armenians and the Government troops, and doubtless excesses
have been committed on both sides. But I am confident that
the [Turkish] nation will soon return to stability and that

it is not in our interest to engage more fully in the matter at the moment."

The termination of the Hamidian massacres occurred in this fashion: At one-thirty on the afternoon of Wednesday, August 26, 1896, a band of two dozen young Armenian activists armed with primitive revolvers and sticks of dynamite walked into the main office of the Ottoman Bank, in Galata, a Christian quarter of Constantinople, across the Golden Horn from the Turkish quarter of Stamboul, and seized the premises. The purpose of the seizure of so visible an institution, the Armenians declared, was to attract the attention of the European powers, who would then compel "constitutional reforms" on the part of Abdul-Hamid. But clearly the Sultan had somehow been apprised of the plan beforehand, for as soon as the Armenians appeared inside the bank, a cordon of Turkish troops arrived to keep the Armenians within the building, sealing them off from the rest of the city. Then, less than an hour after the capture of the bank, mobs of Turks, armed with the same hardwood clubs that had been seen in the country, began storming into Galata. The Turks fell upon Armenians wherever they could find them. In some cases, specific individuals—usually leaders of the professions—were sought after and, when found, were dragged into the street for instant execution. Generally, the mobs roamed through the streets and houses, breaking up shops, clubbing the inhabitants to the ground. For three days, the destruction and killing continued. M. Tissot, an attaché of the French Embassy, wrote in a

letter to *Le Matin* that the soles of his shoes had been sticky
with blood from his walk to the office. A young secretary at
the English Embassy, Henry Graves, wrote in a journal,
which he subsequently published, that he had seen a "mob of
several dozen Turks, among whom were two personal aides
of the Sultan, stamping upon the dead or dying bodies of an
Armenian family." There were reports of disemboweling, of
heads being split by stones, of the rape of small children. An
American clergyman, Dr. George Hepworth, who visited
Constantinople the following year, wrote about this frenzy
of killing for the New York *Herald*:

> It is difficult to obtain the number of those murdered,
> but it is clear that there were quite enough. My informants,
> who are by no means all Armenian, tell me that they lay
> in the streets by the dozen, by the score, and in some places
> by the hundreds. Cold, stark bodies of men who had com-
> mitted no crime. . . . I inquired how the evil work was
> done? "Mostly with clubs," one of my friends answered.
> "There was rarely any noise, no shouting, only the soft
> thudding of the clubs. The Armenians, who had no weap-
> ons, fell like wheat before a scythe." I have often thought
> of the terror of that image: the "soft thudding of the clubs."

An hour or so after the bank's capture, the Armenians
who were now virtual prisoners there, and whose presence
had provided an "official pretext" for what the government
described as a "public protest," began to throw out some of
the dynamite, with a view to attracting European notice and

support. One stick exploded, and damaged a cornice on one of the bank's walls—the falling stones from which were reported to have injured the arm of a Turkish soldier. Apparently moved by the possibility of damage to the bank, its English director, Sir Edgar Vincent, requested the Sultan to give safe-conduct to the young activists. Finally, about midnight, they were permitted to leave the bank and were then convoyed to sanctuary on Sir Edgar's yacht.

For the next couple of days, Turkish mobs took to the streets of the Armenian neighborhoods, and by the end of the rioting the French and English consular attachés estimated that somewhere between five and eight thousand Armenians had been killed. On the morning of August 29, an open telegram, written in French and signed by the major European powers, was delivered to the Sultan. The message said that it was the "advice of the Signatories" that the massacres "must cease immediately." It also stated that "continuance means danger to [the Ottoman] throne and dynasty." That was certainly the right note to strike with Abdul-Hamid. The same day, the command went out from Yildiz Palace, confirmed by the sheikh-ul-Islam, that the Sultan had "forbidden to kill."

I had the illusion of finally beginning to comprehend something important about the Armenians—something that might at least partly explain the peculiarly shrill and wounded quality of the Armenian response to the trauma of the Turkish massacres. For ever since I began my "investigations" of the Armenians I had been perplexed as to why so many of them, even today, still seemed inextricably fixated on the evil times that had befallen their people in Abdul-Hamid's Turkey, and later, in 1915, at the hands of the Young Turks. In a sense, I knew that this was an inexcusably insensitive thing for me to think or write—for me, a comfortable American in the nineteen-seventies, to wonder why my people (or any people) should still respond deeply or with passion to the fact of their countrymen's having been killed in the thousands, in the hundreds of thousands. And yet it was what I wondered.

It had never occurred to me that what happened to the Armenians was *worse* than what had happened to numerous other peoples, nations, creeds in the course of man's long inhumanity to man. What could be worse than death, worse even than death by pain? And was there an appreciable difference to the victim in being hanged, decapitated, clubbed, gassed, or starved, or undergoing any of the other nearly endless methods that men have developed for administering physical pain to one another? Even so, the response of the Armenians to the bygone brutalities of the Turks seemed of a different nature from the response of other groups to massacre. It was as if a particular poison had entered the system several generations back, and had remained within it: a poison that one might up to a point live with but that caused the limbs suddenly to twitch, or the mouth—perhaps in mid-sentence—to grimace grotesquely.

After all, what invisible "virus" was it that had reduced to tears that old man I talked with a few months earlier in New York, on Thirty-third Street, and that had brought so many other Armenians of my acquaintance to the equivalent of gnashing their teeth? What was it that had caused such a marvelously tough writer as William Saroyan to manifest an unearthly sweetness? What had driven my father to write about everything except his Armenian background, and all his life to refuse to weep over anything? What of Sarkis—surely also a tough and rational man—and his wild diatribes against "the Turks"? Some writers, I knew, had ascribed the emotional or ingratiating aspects of the Armenian temperament to the Armenians' long history of being a conquered people. But the main fact to emerge from the lengthy and curious history of the Armenians seemed to be that though much of the time Armenia had been controlled by a greater power, the Armenians themselves had remained independent of mind and spirit. They had been hardy mountain people first, perhaps not very cultured or clever—people who grow up in the mountains are rarely cultured or clever—but direct, practical, and physical. And if the depressing and isolating experience of several centuries of Ottoman Turkish rule had turned the Armenians inward, had sent them down the roads that were then most practical—the roads of trade and commerce, of interpreting, of "being useful"—today one might see for oneself on the streets of Erevan the still direct, clear-eyed, at times quite fierce look of younger Armenians, who were now left (more or less) to pursue their own instincts. No, it was not so simple a matter; one could not "explain" Armenians by saying that they had suffered a great deal, or that they had always suffered a great deal.

In obvious ways, the closest parallel lay with the Jews, who had undergone, numerically, an even larger genocide in Hitler's Germany. But here, too, there seemed to be a difference. Certainly there were many Jews I knew, or knew of, who still looked back to the terrible period of the concentration camps and gas chambers as if it were an open wound, a fact of everyday consciousness. But, for one thing, the Jewish experience in Germany had been fairly recent. For another thing, it seemed to me that a majority of the Jews did not look backward in this way—in the manner of people bearing a permanently open wound. Of course, the issue might be forced: a careless or abrasive remark, sometimes only remotely anti-Semitic in intent, and even the most assimilated American Jew might respond with a flash of anger about the Six Million. Indeed, I had sometimes noticed a curiously proprietary air on the part of Jews and Armenians alike toward the misfortunes of their own peoples—proprietary and almost competitive, in the fashion of two insecure strangers trying to narrate two similar nightmares in an inattentive room. "Now, these Armenians," an intelligent Jewish friend had once said to me, with studied vagueness, "didn't they once have some *trouble* with the Turks?" Another time, I had overheard an Armenian say outright, "The way they talk, you'd think the Jews invented genocide." Doubtless this was original black comedy—perverse and deeply human. But generally it seemed to me that the Jews had handled their nightmare better than the Armenians had handled theirs: had somehow resolved it, or, at least, incorporated the trauma into everyday life—were more nearly free of it.

And what of the countless other peoples who had undergone massacre and genocide: the Ibos of Nigeria; the Communists of Indonesia; the Hindus of Bangladesh; the Incas of South America; the Indians of North America; the Ukrainian peasants of the U.S.S.R.; the black slaves of Haiti and Guadeloupe; the Protestants; the Catholics; the Muslims; the Cappadocians whom Tigran of Armenia had marched across the wilderness to his new capital; and all the rest, whose names and stories were never entered, or entered vividly enough, in history books—for the list is surely long and ancient? Had not all these suffered, and suffered very greatly? What, then, was different about the Armenian experience? Perhaps it had not been so different? Perhaps some peoples were created with more self-pity, shrillness, and vulnerability than other peoples? It seemed an unlikely proposition. I thought of something I had increasingly noticed in Armenians: an absence of a profoundly convincing "flash of anger"—at least, in this matter of their feelings against the Turks. An absence of a rage that *they* seemed to believe in. Or maybe it was not so much an absence of rage as a rerouting: a rage trapped underground. Beneath the skin.

I THOUGHT of my father often in those days, for I was conscious of many things about him: conscious, for example, that he was born in 1896, the final year of Abdul-Hamid's massacres, and had never talked about any of this in my presence; conscious that, to that degree, he had tried to free me. It seemed no small thing to have tried to free a son from one's own pain. There was also something about it of the story of the man and the fox: the man who, for fear of being caught with contraband, clutches the animal so close beneath his shirt that the animal tears at his stomach.

It was hard to imagine what this pain had been. The pain of being hated—hated unto death. For what was genocide except an expression of generalized hate, a hate so wide and encompassing that it included everyone—man, woman, child—within a certain national or racial group? If a "crime of passion" was particularizing—*you* stole *my* wife—at least it defined the victim as himself. Genocide not only killed its victims but dehumanized them, in the ultimate sense of ignoring the particulars that had made each one individual: save only the most basic and unindividual of all characteristics—the supposedly racial.

I wondered what *his* father had told him about the massacres, about Abdul-Hamid, about the Turks. A certain amount, I imagined. Probably rather more than he—an uncertain Armenian-English youth—had wished to hear. "Your grandfather," an elderly Armenian once told me, "was very active in Armenian affairs." Sometimes it was hard to believe that my father had had a father—this more distant father I had never seen.

My father was born in Bulgaria, where his family had been settled for several generations. Before that, the Kouyoumjians had been in Constantinople. Before that, they had lived in the ancient city of Ani, on the Armenian plateau. In the town of Rustchuk, in Bulgaria, the Kouyoumjians owned and ran a department store—the Kouyoumjian store. It had been described to me only a short while before by the aged grandmother of a school friend of my daughter's, who remembered it from her childhood. "A very fine place," she said to me reassuringly. "You could buy everything there."

The Kouyoumjian store. The man in the blue velvet hat. Some odd memories of my childhood came back to me. I remembered my father standing on the lawn of our house and telling me that I should learn how to box, how to defend myself. I think he used the phrase "self-defense." I was eight years old at the time and had given no thought to "self-defense"—at least, not beyond what basic skills were required to scuffle with the neighbor children. He had his hands on his hips and wore a white shirt and white trousers. Perhaps he had been playing tennis. I think he even briefly struck a boxing pose and made a show of sparring with me. I was a most reluctant partner. "You have to know how to defend yourself," he said, with surprising severity. He seemed very intense about— I never knew what. Boxing? We never talked about it afterward.

What had Miss Haslip written in her book *The Sultan?* "The Armenians . . . with a courage which belied their reputation, succeeded in beating off the [Hamidiyeh] attack."

My father was a short man, although wiry, and carried himself with a certain brittle strength. I believe I remember his saying once, "All Armenians are short." (There are no piano tuners in Japan. All Swedes are drunks.) It made me weep inside my head to think of him sometimes. That figure in the white shirt and white trousers, hands on hips. That figure whom I later saw inside his coffin, wearing some appropriate suit, the necktie well in place, everything motionless, the impassivity a final fact. I used to think that what he had wanted of me had been hard. But what he had wanted of himself turned out to have been literally unspeakable.

We were at Sarkis's house one evening, having supper and supposedly engaging in a "discussion of international literature." First, let me describe his house, for we had not been there before. His wife had been "down with the grippe," he had explained on several occasions, although I had hardly pestered him for an invitation. The main thing I think one would want to say about it is that it was rough-hewn and small (or, from another point of view, sturdy and compact), and occupied a pleasant plot of ground perhaps two miles outside Erevan, on the far side of the olive-green hills. The house was at the end of a dirt road (for the countryside seemed to start up right at the outskirts), which was lined with tall trees and dusty shrubs and was in every respect rural, except that one could glimpse two or three new, pink stone apartment buildings through the trees, barely a half mile away. All the same, there was a feeling about the area of tranquillity, and small gardens, and lazily barking dogs. "As you see, we are in the suburbs!" exclaimed Sarkis. He was clearly pleased with himself in his role as host. He showed us his garden—a tiny plot that contained mostly dirt, but where a few purple flowers and green shoots struggled through the light-brown soil. "I always tell myself that I must work in the garden on weekends," said Sarkis, "but I never do." The house was fashioned of gray stone, somewhat in the manner of a peasant house, and the outside was not especially lovely. There was a tin roof and a weather-worn wooden porch, with several very old chairs set against the wall. "You can't imagine how many rubles I had to pay for all this," said Sarkis, "and I will never tell you. But it is charming, is it not? Imagine living in an apartment building when one could live in such a house!" Inside were three small rooms, like boxes, on the ground floor and, presumably, a few more small rooms upstairs. Everything was spotless and in order, with lacelike covers on the armrests of the faded sofa, and numerous tinted family photographs in oval frames set out on the polished side tables. The whole effect was rather Victorian. Sarkis's wife appeared: a cheerful-seeming, dark-haired woman, slightly younger than her husband. She was shy as to language, but she shook hands cordially and did not appear shy about anything else. Nor did she seem to have suffered much from the grippe.

We sat around a shining dark-wood table in the small living room and consumed quantities of shashlik and green onions; also Armenian pastries, newly baked, and black, smoking coffee, and brandy out of a bottle obviously not often used, which Sarkis produced from a cupboard, set before us, beamed at, and began to pour seigneurially. In one corner of the room stood a large—or, rather, thick—wooden television set, itself quite Victorian, and beside it, against the wall, was a display chest, made of the same shining wood as the table, and containing plates and pinkish glassware.

"The crystal is from Czechoslovakia," said Sarkis. "My wife admires it, although I don't see what is wrong with our Soviet glassware."

His wife said something to him in Armenian, and he laughed.

"She says the Soviet glassware is no good," he said. "Imagine that such a statement should be made in my own house!" He laughed again and poured some more brandy.

We had many toasts: to Ararat, to Armenia, to America, to friendship between our two peoples. "I wish my son were here," said Sarkis. "He is nearby at the university, but he never comes home. That is the way with sons, is it not? He makes this joke all the time: 'I have to work hard, Papa, so that I won't have to teach English to high-school students.' But he is a brilliant boy." I tried to imagine what Sarkis's son might look like. He got up and showed us a photograph: Sarkis and a thin young man standing in sunlight beside a low hedge—perhaps on the dirt road outside. The boy (for even at nineteen or twenty he still seemed a boy) had a grave, sweet expression on his face and stood nearly a head taller than his father, who had his arm around his son's waist, as if holding on. Respect thy father! We drank a toast to Sarkis's son.

After dinner, two of Sarkis's friends (or, as he insisted, "colleagues") came by—Arshil, a youngish man with a pale face and eyeglasses, who also taught English at the high school, and Kevork, an older man, thickset, with thick hands and a coarse face, who was a member of the local Writers' Union. It had been Sarkis's notion that we should meet to discuss the literature of our two countries, but from the start it was clear that the emphasis was to be on American writers.

"Of course, it is hard to obtain translations," said Kevork, lighting up an evil-looking brown cigarette, "but it does not seem to be a high time in American literature."

"Which American writers most interest you?" I asked the two colleagues.

"I have read both Jerome Salinger and Scott Fitzgerald," said Arshil. "This year, I have read the story of Gatsby."

"I find both writers childish," said Kevork.

"Yes, Fitzgerald is undeniably childish about capitalism," said Sarkis. "But you must agree that he is an excellent writer of short novels."

"A great writer must write more than short novels," said Kevork.

Arshil said that he had also read Walt Whitman, John Steinbeck, and Edgar Poe. Sarkis and Arshil discussed Walt Whitman and Stephen Crane. It was strange to be gossiping about so many dead writers.

Kevork remarked that he preferred Dostoevsky to Edgar Poe. "Edgar Poe is a miniaturist," he said.

"Of course, Poe is not as serious as Dostoevsky," said Arshil.

I made the mistake of asking about Solzhenitsyn, partly

lulled by the warmth of the brandy, and doubtless also out of sheer hostility to Kevork, who seemed exactly the sort of person who might have made trouble for him. In what I meant to be a harmless, literary manner, I said, "How do you compare a modern writer such as Solzhenitsyn, who deals in large themes, with classical writers such as Tolstoy or Dostoevsky?"

There was the proverbial moment of silence.

"Nobody can be compared with Tolstoy," said Sarkis.

Then Kevork spoke. He looked not at me but toward the floor. "Solzhenitsyn is a special case," he said. "He is a national writer, a national writer of talent. But he is one who chose to abuse his talent with self-service." He looked around at all of us. "Besides, if a writer wishes to attack his country, then he should not expect to be honored by it."

There was another moment of silence. I thought Sarkis seemed pained, and I felt bad about having brought up the subject, or perhaps about having brought it up so trivially. Arshil got up from his chair and poured everyone some more brandy. He seemed a kind man, with many obscure feelings, and probably not very forceful—the traditional high-school English teacher. Now he said, "In America, would you say that the hippies are still a serious problem?"

"There are few hippies any more," my wife said.

"Everybody must have a job and do productive work," said Sarkis. "Is that not so?"

"In Armenia there are no hippies," said Arshil.

There was a prim, genteel quality to the conversation—

almost "un-Armenian," it occurred to me. Then I thought, Whose idea was it, anyway, that Armenians were somehow picturesque or offbeat? Surely all along they had been so palpably, doggedly, almost pathetically straight. Through one of Sarkis's small windows, the lights of a tall building blinked in the distance. It seemed all too plausible that the kings of Nairi had built those solid pink apartment houses.

We talked for a while longer about novels and novelists. There was something cheerfully indiscriminate in the other men's tastes—an absence of modishness, of topical shading. It made one think of the way a starving man might overlook the need for spices. I remember Arshil's saying at one point that in Moscow two years earlier he had bought two books by "the novelist H. Robbins," and had found them "vigorous but insensitive."

Then Kevork rose to his feet, excused himself shyly, and said that he must return home. He shook hands all around. "Someday, I should like to visit America," he said to me.

My wife asked, "Where would you most like to go?"

"I have heard of the Widener Library at Harvard," he said. "I should like to go there. Also to Niagara Falls."

After he had left, we sat together in the living room. Sarkis said, not unkindly, "You should not have asked him about Solzhenitsyn."

"I know that," I said. "I'm sorry."

"It's all right," said Sarkis.

"I thought things were more relaxed," I said.

"Yes," said Sarkis.

Arshil said, "Four months ago, the police took away his son."

I looked at Sarkis, who was staring at the carpet. His wife stood in the doorway to the kitchen drying a glass. "That is true," he said. "Yes, those things also happen." He looked up at us. "Young men do foolish things, do they not?" he said. And "Young men are crazy!" For a second, he seemed close to tears. Then he said, "Come. I will show you my library."

We all followed him up some narrow stairs into a small room, apparently adjoining an equally small bedroom. Its walls were tiers of bookshelves jammed with books. The books were mostly English and American, some French, quite a few Armenian, the majority of them ancient—or, anyway, well-thumbed—paperbacks with titles ranging from *A Farewell to Arms* to the *Sunset Barbecue Cook Book*. "You see, I take whatever I can find," said Sarkis.

"It's a wonderful library," said my wife.

Arshil held up a loose-leaf ledger, filled with names and dates. "He lends us all books," said Arshil, and suddenly he hugged Sarkis.

My thoughts were still on Kevork and his son—though I was aware not so much of this nameless, faceless boy, this "foolish young man" (had he, too, been photographed with a grave, sweet expression?), or even of his father, who had not wished to be made to express himself on Solzhenitsyn, as of all the other dark corners in the lives of these people: Sarkis, Arshil, Arak, doubtless Vartan, all the rest.

I said to Sarkis when we were back downstairs, "How is it that so many hard things have happened to Armenians everywhere, and yet it is still the Turks they hate so much?"

Sarkis looked at me evenly, his composure recovered. "Because they killed so many of our people. Your people and my people."

For a moment, I felt I might hit him, beat at him with my fists. There was something so confining in that thought. Then I felt ridiculous and embarrassed. All evening, I had wanted to embrace him.

Sarkis's wife came up and gave us a small package of her pastries to take back to our hotel. She stood in the low doorway of the little house, her hand briefly in Sarkis's. She shook our hands again. Goodbye, goodbye.

Arshil and Sarkis walked with us down the dirt road toward the bus stop. The night was clear and fragrant, with half a moon above the hills. An invisible dog barked far away. The great trees rose overhead, dark shapes against the blue-black sky. Arshil walked along beside me. Ahead I could vaguely hear Sarkis telling my wife some amusing story about the building of his house. How he had tried to fix the roof, or build the roof. His voice rose and fell in the warm night.

Arshil said quietly, "Do you know what I think was worst about the trouble with the Turks? It was that the Turks and the Armenians were brothers."

I said, "But I thought the Turks hated the Armenians."

"Don't brothers sometimes hate one another?" said

Arshil. In the dim light (from the moon? from a distant street lamp?), he seemed to be smiling, but I imagined that his face was often set that way. "Now and then, my grand-mother used to speak of those times," he said. "You know, in 1915, or perhaps 1916, after my grandfather was killed in the great massacre, she fled here from Van. In wintertime, too. She was a hard old lady."

"What happened to your grandfather?" I asked.

"He was a doctor," said Arshil. "He was also in one of the resistance bands that used to attack the Turkish convoys. Of course, they caught them finally and brought them to the square where they were to be hanged. But first they were beaten—beaten terribly, I can well believe. I can still remember my grandmother's voice as she used to say, 'But the man who gave the worst beatings was Djebal, our neighbor, Aram's patient—a man whose wife he had saved from the typhus.' "

"What are you two talking about?" said Sarkis as we reached the main highway.

"History," said Arshil.

"It's too nice an evening for history," said Sarkis.

We stood together beneath the street lamp waiting for the bus to come.

"Was it not a fine evening?" Sarkis said. "I think even our English teacher is pleased." He embraced Arshil. "Do we not live well?" he said.

Soon, a bus appeared out of the dark. Sarkis stayed by the open door as we climbed aboard.

"We are friends!" he called from the street.

"We are friends," I said.

Behind us, Sarkis and Arshil stood in the pool of yellow light, arms around each other, waving. Brothers.

On the subject of brotherhood, at least this much was true of Constantinople in the summer of 1908, when the Young Turks took over control of the Ottoman government from the declining and elderly Abdul-Hamid II. In the words of the British historian Bernard Lewis: "The long night of Hamidian despotism was over; the dawn of freedom had come. The constitution had once again been proclaimed and elections ordered. Turks and Armenians embraced in the streets."

The popular Turkish poet Tevfik Fikret, whose work had often been suppressed for its anti-Hamidian views, poured out his enthusiasm as follows:

> Now we are far from that accursed night. . . .
> Our eyes have opened to a radiant morning.

Some years later, after the debacle of the First World War and the eventual collapse of the Young Turk government, an American journalist, H. G. Dwight, who had been in Turkey during that period of hope and wishful thinking, wrote in a book about Constantinople: "Although time has only partially fulfilled so many generous aspirations, or has turned them to bitterness, I refuse to believe that they were totally insincere. I shall always count it, on the contrary, among the most enlarging experiences of my life to have been in Constantinople in 1908, and to have seen a people at one of those rare moments when it really lives."

From many accounts, there was literally dancing in the streets during the midsummer weeks, and if Turks and Armenians embraced, small wonder, for the "long night of Hamidian despotism" did appear to be over. Abdul-Hamid himself was still sultan, but he was no longer an autocrat. The cause for celebration was the relatively bloodless coup d'état whereby units of the Ottoman Army controlled by the Young Turks had compelled the Sultan to restore the constitution—the same modestly liberal instrument that he had pulled out of a hat in 1876 and then abandoned. However, Turkish political life had changed since the more innocent days of 1876 and the Yeni Osmanlilar—the nineteenth-century Young Turks, with their romantic, Europe-inspired constitutional-reform movement. The men who made the revolution of 1908 belonged to a more recent and far more authoritarian Turkish political party, called the Committee of Union and Progress (Ittihad ve Terakki). Furthermore, they were mostly from the military wing of the Committee—disaffected junior officers of Ottoman Third Army units in Macedonia. For another thing, in the ten-year interval since Abdul-Hamid's massacre of the Armenians an important split had developed between Turkish and Armenian reformers, who nonetheless continued to meet together regularly until 1913, in an attempt to reconcile their diverging aims.

Essentially, the chief source of disagreement between the Turks and the Armenians was the issue of European intervention. For ever since the Hamidian massacres the Armenians (notably the members of the political party Dashnaktsutiun) had felt that the best possibilities for reform lay in the intervention of liberal Europe, whose leaders continued to profess concern and sympathy over the "Armenian Question"—needless to say, without having done much of anything about it. The Turks, on the other hand, had become more and more hostile to the notion of imposing European political ideas on ancient Turkish Islamic life. Thus, just as the Armenians (who had recently lost an eighth of their population to the paranoia and displeasure of Abdul-Hamid) were looking increasingly to Europe for guarantees of safety and political reform, the Turkish political and military activists were growing steadily anti-European (chiefly anti-English and anti-French), and turning more nationalistically Turkish and Islamic in their plans for a new nation. But even after the 1908 coup neither the Turks nor the Armenians had any very radical program for the old Ottoman empire, which both groups still conceived of in its traditional form, including the sultanate.

Such solemn and almost shy ambitions—the shyness of political children! In our starker and more violent century (a Lear among centuries), scarcely a political manifesto has

been issued that does not have the smell of murder somewhere about it. Years after the genocide of the Armenians in
Turkey during the First World War, some would say that
the Armenians had been trying to secede from Turkey—and
by the time of the genocide to some extent that was true. But
in 1908, far from wishing to break away from, or even over-
turn, this backward and bankrupt "empire," they seem to
have wanted mainly to regenerate it, and piously, in the
manner of self-absorbed children, worried that someone
might misunderstand and think they wished to do away
with the office of sultan, to take that step so final in any
family—parricide, regicide, sultanicide.

But time never stays still for anyone, perhaps least of all
for reformer-revolutionaries. In April 1909, after the dancing
in the streets of Constantinople had died down, Abdul-
Hamid (whose telegraph system had provided him with
such inferior information concerning the coup d'état) attempted a last maneuver. Still in Yildiz Palace and still sultan, knowing that the Young Turks were tinged with
liberalism (although very slightly so) and that any liberalism implied religious liberalism, even secularism—which
had traditionally been anathema to the conservative rural
Turks of the provinces—Abdul-Hamid, together with the
conservative priesthood and reactionary elements in the
Army, concocted a counter-revolution. For a short while, the
new government was in danger of falling. Muslim dissidents
gathered in Saint Sophia Square chanting, "The Holy Law
is in danger!" Several Army garrisons in Anatolia, protest-

ing that they did not wish to be governed by "college-trained officers," threatened to march on the capital. But the Young Turks still controlled the majority of the troops, and the counter-revolution was quelled.

Thus, Abdul-Hamid was finally deposed and sent into exile in Salonika, taking with him but a few retainers and only four members of his harem, the rest of which was disbanded, with the women (many of them of mature age) left to be called for by parents or relatives—who now came in from remote sections of the country—in the fashion of schoolchildren being picked up at the end of term. A new sultan was installed, but merely as a figurehead. The Young Turks were firmly in power, having perhaps learned an early lesson: never to underestimate the religious conservatism and fervor of their countrymen. If Turkey should be for the Turks, then it was worth remembering that the Turks were still predominantly and passionately Muslim.

CONSIDER SOME snapshots of the Young Turks who ruled Turkey on the eve of the First World War. They were taken by an official Ottoman photographer and reprinted in an *Illustrated London News* of 1913:

The first man has a large head, with a round, heavy face. He is forty-one years old, but he looks much older—middle-aged. There is a fringe of dark beard around his chin, and on the whole he seems to have a sober, almost bureaucratic expression, which belies his braided uniform. He is Jemal

Pasha, once a colonel in the Third Army, now Minister of Marine.

The second man is different. He is short, slender, with a decidedly Gallic look to him. He has a thin, trim mustache and dark, carefully brushed-back hair. His face is fine-boned, with intense eyes. There is something of the dandy in his appearance. He is Enver Pasha, thirty-two years old, formerly a major in the Third Army, now Minister of War.

The third man is from the same mold as the first: a round and heavy Turkish face, with ample cheeks and a bearded chin. His eyes seem more alert than Jemal's, and more concentrated than Enver's. There is something even of a professor in his gaze—but a rough-hewn, almost coarse professor. He is Talaat Pasha, forty-one years old, formerly a telegraph clerk in Edirne, now Minister of the Interior.

TURKEY for the Turks. Once the Young Turks were in charge of the country, they struggled with such noble matters as "land reform" and a reorganization of the Constantinople Fire Department. The Young Turk government also solved the long-standing problem of the roaming dog packs of Constantinople. It collected all the stray dogs of the city and shipped them to a deserted island in the Sea of Marmara, where in due course they starved to death.

Nor did the great powers now choose to sit around for very long placidly observing the new government, in the fashion of benign uncles looking upon a small child. In

1908, Austria-Hungary, with Russian approval, dived into the Turkish European provinces and extracted Bosnia and Herzegovina. In the same year, with Austria-Hungary's approval, Bulgaria declared its independence. In 1911, Italy, with the endorsement of France and England, acquired the Ottoman North African province of Tripoli. In 1912, Greece, Serbia, and Bulgaria formed a loose confederacy and pushed Turkey almost completely out of the Balkans. Indeed, on the eve of the First World War, Turkey's best friend appeared to be Germany.

For perhaps thirty years before the war, Germany had made no secret of its special fondness for Turkey—a fondness that could easily be explained as the desire of a belatedly colonial, modern state to exploit the considerable economic possibilities of the unindustrialized Ottoman empire. Twice —in 1889 and 1898—Kaiser Wilhelm himself had traveled by yacht to Constantinople, where he had stoutly shaken the hand of Abdul-Hamid, kissed him on both cheeks, and been shown at least a small degree of affection in return. German track had been laid down for the Berlin-Baghdad Railway. A German telephone system had been installed in Constantinople. In 1913, the year before the outbreak of war in Europe, the Young Turk government accepted a detachment of German "military advisers," under General Otto Liman von Sanders, who were attached to the Turkish Army with a view to instructing and training it in new techniques.

In the summer of 1914, however, as the World War crept

closer, with the swift moves of Germany and the great mobilizations of the Entente powers, Germany was not eager to have Turkey come in on its behalf. The Kaiser felt that Turkey's armed forces were too ill-equipped and disorganized to be of much use in a military alliance. Perversely, it was some of the more ambitious Young Turks, notably Enver Pasha, who pushed the matter, for evidently they wished to be allies of mighty Germany in the great adventure that was just beginning. On August 2, a secret military alliance with Germany was signed, which left Turkey with only the appearance of neutrality. England then forced the issue by impounding two Turkish warships that were under construction in English yards. In retaliation, Turkey permitted two German warships in flight across the Mediterranean to seek refuge in Turkish waters. England, France, and Russia demanded the immediate disarming of the German warships and the repatriation of their crews. At first, the Young Turks hesitated, and then they announced that they had "purchased" the warships from the Germans. On October 29, the two ships, still manned with German crews under a German commander but flying the Turkish flag, attacked Russian shipping and ports in the Black Sea, and shortly thereafter Russia declared war on Turkey. The Ottoman empire was finally in the war, on the side of Germany.

Why should the Young Turks have been so eager to bring their impoverished and backward country into the World War? It is hard to say. Economically as well as militarily, the Turks were in poor shape when they entered the

war, and they were a good deal worse off when it was over.
On the other hand, one might ask what rational basis any of
the more advanced nations had for entering that wretched
war, with its self-destructive eruption of dammed-up aggres-
sions. Doubtless, in the dim mind of each nation there existed a kind of dream: *Drang nach Osten;* Ruling the
Waves; *La Gloire;* Pan-Slavism. In the case of the Young
Turks, it seems to have been a dream (albeit a vague and
hazy one, like all their dreams) of a new Turkish empire,
which would incorporate the Muslim population of southern Russia and also the Muslims of Iran and Egypt: a pan-
Muslim empire.

In any event, with much of the civilized world resound-
ing to such hunting calls as "On to Paris!" and "On to
Berlin!" how is one to blame Enver Pasha—still a young
man, full of odd bravadoes and conceits—for mounting his
own cavalry charge toward "the East"? Which is to say that
soon after Turkey was officially in the war Enver Pasha,
Minister of War for the Ottoman empire, took passage with
a small staff across the Black Sea to Trebizond; from there
rode eastward into the Turkish Armenian provinces where
he rounded up all the available troops of the Turkish Ninth
Army; and then headed northeast into the Russian Caucasus. Precisely where he was going, nobody knows—and
nobody knew then. In the manner of Darius the Great, he
was possessed of some grand intuitive "northern vision."
General Liman von Sanders had strongly advised against
the enterprise—whatever it might be—and he was right.

Enver, at the head of a column of one hundred thousand hastily assembled Turkish soldiers, most of them still wearing summer uniforms, enjoyed a few well-acclaimed initial victories, surprising some Russian detachments and capturing several villages. But in short order the situation fell apart. The Russians reorganized and counterattacked en masse. Besides, Enver had chosen to conduct this campaign in what was now the early Russian winter, and great numbers of his troops began to succumb to frostbite and disease. By the first week in January 1915, the Turkish Ninth Army had been virtually wiped out, and Enver—unusually subdued and sullen—returned to Constantinople.

In the middle of that month, Jemal Pasha led another Turkish army, including a company of whirling dervishes, south toward Egypt. Jemal's force reached the Suez with very little difficulty, but upon encountering the British, opposite Ismailia, they were thrown back. From the start, there was little logic anywhere in the Turkish military position, with slight vitality in the ill-equipped troops and few resources at home. The dream had apparently been of short duration and now seemed to be over. Enver, in Constantinople, went to his office each morning and, sitting behind his desk, attended to paperwork. He refused to discuss the Russian campaign with anyone. Jemal had fallen back to Syria, his army now in the role of a defensive garrison. Then, late in April 1915, the English, assisted by a force of Australians and New Zealanders, landed at Gallipoli.

A student of the drama might say that at this point the

stage was set for a variety of possible dénouements. Turkey might be swiftly forced out of the war by the Allied landing. Or the Young Turk government might be overthrown, either from outside or from within—for there was increasing dissatisfaction with the adventurous but unsuccessful pashas on the part of the conservative faction in the country, especially out in the provinces, where the lot of the poor Turkish farmer had become even worse as a result of war taxation. Consider the situation for a moment: Enver and Jemal—the warriors—were on the defensive in Constantinople and Syria. The hated English were on the doorstep in the Dardanelles, where they were opposed by sixty thousand Turkish troops under General Liman von Sanders and his second-in-command, an early leader of the Young Turk movement named Mustafa Kemal. And then there was the matter of the Armenians.

For immediately after the outbreak of the war both sides had made special efforts to gain the support of the Armenians, inasmuch as the Armenian mountain plateau was considered as strategically valuable in the twentieth century as it had been in ancient times. Perhaps more so. Not only did it represent a "buffer" between Russia and Turkey but its mountainous and central position made it a key to the Black Sea, and even to the northern access to India. Furthermore, since the great oil discoveries of the eighteen-nineties Armenia's proximity to both the Russian fields at Baku, on the Caspian Sea, and the English wells in Mesopotamia had made the region an object of marked interest to most of the great powers. In the autumn of 1914, Count Vorontsov-Dashkov, viceroy of the Transcaucasian provinces, promised the Russian Armenians on behalf of the czar that if they should unreservedly support Russia in the war, then after the war Russia would grant autonomy to the six Turkish-Armenian provinces. At about the same time, in Turkish Armenia, officials from the Young Turk government appeared at a Dashnak convention in Erzurum and promised the delegates that if they should unreservedly support Turkey, then after the war the Turkish government would grant all Armenians autonomy in a "Turkish protectorate" to be made up of certain of the Russian-Armenian provinces as well as parts of the Turkish provinces of Erzurum, Van, and Bitlis.

Now, one should point out that the Ottoman law that had forbidden Armenians to serve in the Turkish armed forces (a restriction that to modern minds might seem like an exemption from death but to earlier minds often seemed more like an exclusion from manhood) had been suspended by 1912, when the Turks needed soldiers for the Balkan War. Many Armenians had then begun to serve in the Turkish Army, and a number of them had been praised for their heroism by Enver Pasha. In fact, at the time that the Young Turks at Erzurum were asking for unreserved support, full conscription was in effect throughout the Ottoman empire, and Armenian men between the ages of twenty and forty-five were already serving in the Turkish armed forces. At Erzurum, therefore, the Armenians replied that those of them who were Turkish subjects would continue to behave in uniform as Turkish subjects; as in the Balkan War, they would do as they were commanded. But the Turkish officials wished for something more. They wanted the Dashnakists to recruit a special Turkish-Armenian detachment, whose purpose would be to fight the Russians on its own and liberate Russian Armenia. This the Dashnakists said they would not do.

Into our dramatic equation, then, one must add the refusal of the Armenians—not yet twenty years after the Hamidian massacres—to put together a special brigade with which to make war against a Christian country that had traditionally expressed sympathy for their cause; and one must also add what, specifically, they were quite agreeable to doing: namely, being conscripted into the Turkish Army, putting on the coarse, dun-colored uniforms and puttees, and being shipped to various barracks in Anatolia, where many of them had already begun their training.

There was another factor that one should not ignore—the so-called Armenian Volunteers. These were a loosely organized collection of irregulars—most of them Russian Armenians recruited from the Tiflis and Erevan branches of Dashnaktsutiun—who served in the early days of the war on the Caucasian front, sometimes as scouts or advance units, more often in guerrilla squads of a dozen or so men, and who engaged in raiding forays against the Turkish troops. The active number of these Volunteers rarely exceeded one thousand (not a sizable force compared to Enver's army of one hundred thousand), but they knew the terrain, and they fought well, and—perhaps more to the point in the Turkish view—they existed. As with many guerrilla operations in our own era, a situation of paranoia and rigidity seems to have prevailed in Turkish official minds whereby merely the idea of such a group—of such an unasked-for and impertinent entity—evoked a specter of rebellious Armenian legions. The Armenians, too, recognized that these Volunteers existed; and their occasional guerrilla raids into the northern sector of Turkish Armenia were regarded by the local inhabitants, variously, as heroic or unsettling. Some photographs of these Volunteers remain, collected in a book, *The Memoirs of Rouben Der Minasian:* amateur snapshots of different bands of ten or twelve men, each group posed formally and rather quaintly, almost in the manner of an eighteen-nineties football team—the men usually with mustaches and fierce expressions, wearing lamb's-wool mountain hats, and carrying bandoliers of cartridges. Der Minasian himself was one of the early leaders of this resistance movement, as were such Armenian heroes as Kevork Chavoush, Aram of Moush, and Andranik. There is a picture of Der Minasian: a man in a wool hat, perhaps twenty or twenty-two, brandishing a grenade as he kneels at the front of a group of guerrillas. There are also numerous accounts of ambushes and escapades, of Turkish platoons and sometimes companies engaged, of nighttime rides and river crossings, villages defended, supply trains looted, exchanges of rifle fire. "At the outskirts of the village of S., I ordered the people to scatter, everyone for himself. I was now all alone with my company of twenty-two, and the dying Kevork. I took stock of the situation and saw that we were securely hemmed in in a tight triangle. On one side was the village of B., crawling with soldiers. On the other side were the swollen waters of the Euphrates." Much bravery, foolhardiness, and youth.

The Volunteers had originally been formed in order to catch the eye of England and France, the two Allies who would soon be so near, in the Dardanelles, and remain so far. But the strongest impression they seem to have made was on the hard-pressed and suspicious Turks. In December 1914, when Enver's ill-fated northern expedition had already begun to falter, a company-strength unit of Volunteers stationed in the snowbound Keri Pass on one occasion held off an entire Turkish division long enough to permit a trapped Russian force to escape. The story was not reported in the distant European press, which in any case was preoccupied with matters on the Western front. But after Enver had returned in defeat to Constantinople, in early 1915, the account began to be noised about in Turkish government circles—and was picked up by the German Embassy—that the chief reason for the failure of the Turkish advance had been "mass defections" of Turkish Armenians to the Russian side. Moreover, a short while later—toward the end of

April 1915—an "incident" took place in the predominantly Armenian town of Van, in eastern Turkey.

ACCORDING TO an American, Grace Knapp, who was in Van at the time, visiting the medical mission, and who later provided a lengthy eyewitness report, the trouble arose shortly after the Governor General of the province of Van, Djevdet Bey, who was a brother-in-law of Enver Pasha, returned from the ill-starred Caucasian campaign. First, on the pretext of asking for their cooperation, he arranged for the murder of four Armenian leaders. Then Turkish troops were instructed to dig entrenchments around the Armenian sector of the town. "On Tuesday, the 20th of April, at 6 A.M., some Turkish soldiers tried to seize one of a band of village women on their way to the city," wrote Miss Knapp. "She fled. Two Armenian soldiers came up and asked the Turks what they were doing. The Turkish soldiers fired on the Armenians, killing them. Thereupon the Turkish entrenchments opened fire. The siege had begun." The Turks had artillery and around four thousand soldiers. "The Armenian force consisted of 1,500 trained riflemen possessing only about 300 rifles. . . . They began to make bullets and cartridges." The Armenians of Van held off the Turks for five weeks, until advancing Russian troops diverted the Turks' attention. Meanwhile, the Turks had massacred most of the Armenians in the surrounding villages and had destroyed much of the Armenian section of Van. "There will either be nothing but Turks or nothing but Armenians left in this city," Djevdet Bey had said on one occasion. In Constantinople, where the foreign press and diplomatic corps had little knowledge of or interest in remote eastern Turkey, the German Embassy sent this dispatch to Berlin: "The Turkish Government has informed us of an attack by armed Armenian insurrectionists on Muslim inhabitants of the town of Van. Many Muslims have been slain. The Turkish Government has been forced to take steps to put down the rebellion." The dramatic equation, whatever its seemingly random or unconnected components, appeared to be in the process of resolution.

"A decree went forth that all Armenians should be disarmed. The Armenians in the [Turkish] Army were drafted out of the fighting ranks, reformed into special labor battalions, and set to work throwing up fortifications and constructing roads." So reads an excerpt from what is probably the most substantial report on the Armenian genocide, *The Treatment of Armenians in the Ottoman Empire, 1915–16,* which was published in London in 1916 under the signature of Viscount James Bryce. Bryce, then an old man, was one of those noble establishment figures—a statesman and scholar, at one time or another Regius Professor of Civil Law at Oxford, President of the Board of Trade, Chief Secretary for Ireland, Undersecretary of State for Foreign Affairs, Chancellor of the Duchy of Lancaster, and Ambassador to Washington. He had once climbed Mt. Ararat, and had been a friend of Gladstone's. The book is an immense undertaking, running to nearly six hundred pages of case histories and eyewitness accounts, and its assembly was the work not of Viscount Bryce but of a young Oxford graduate. "I had the good fortune," wrote Viscount Bryce in a prefatory note, "to secure the cooperation of a young historian of high academic distinction, Mr. Arnold J. Toynbee, late Fellow of Balliol College, Oxford. He undertook to examine and put together the pieces of evidence collected." The Bryce-Toynbee report (Professor Toynbee today is several years older than Bryce was in 1916, and is the possessor of a parallel eminence) continues: "The disarming of the civil population was left to the local authorities, and in every administrative centre a reign of terror began. The authorities demanded the production of a definite number of arms. Those who could not produce them were tortured, often in fiendish ways; those who procured them for surrender, by purchase from their Muslim neighbours or by other means, were imprisoned for conspiracy against the Government. Few of these were young men, for most of the young had been called up to serve."

From an *Address delivered in America, 13th December, 1915, by a professor from the college at X.:* "Persons suspected [of keeping arms] were arrested and taken to the Government Building, where they were subjected to the cruelest forms of torture. Usually they were bound and bastinadoed until they became unconscious. Boiling water was sometimes poured on the soles of the feet, to increase the pain of the bastinadoing. . . . At least two men of our city died under this torture. . . . They took [the blacksmith] to the Government Building. There they bound him, and four brutal men stuffed his mouth with filth, and beat him with rods all over the body until he became unconscious. As soon as he regained consciousness, they repeated the process. . . .

We learned afterward that the occasion for this man's torture was that he was seen casting a 16-lb. shot, which we had ordered him to make for our college field-day sports this year. The man who saw him reported to the police that he had been making bombs."

From a *Narrative of an Armenian lady departed from C.:* "The Turkish officials searched the Armenian churches and schools of G., H., C., AQ., AR., AS., and the surrounding villages, but without finding anything incriminating. . . . After that, they arrested from the town of C. the following persons: Professor B., Mr. H., and his brother J. . . . as well as many others old and young. . . . They took them to the house of V. Agha, stripped them one by one, and gave them 300 lashes on their backs. When they fainted, they threw them into a stable and waited until they had revived, in order to beat them again. . . . After beating T. Effendi in H. and tearing out his fingernails and the flesh of his hands and feet they put a rope under his arms, dragged him to C., and threw him into prison."

From a *Narrative of a foreign resident of German nationality:* "I was called to a house one day where I saw a sheet which originated from the prison, and which was being sent to the wash. This sheet was covered with blood, and running in long streams. I was also shown clothes which were drenched and exceedingly dirty. It was a puzzle to me what they could possibly have done to the prisoners, but I got to the bottom of the matter by the help of two very reliable persons who witnessed part of it themselves.

"The prisoner is put in a room . . . and gendarmes standing in twos at both sides . . . administer bastinadoes, each in their turn, as long as they have enough force in them. In Roman times forty strokes were administered at the very most; in this place, however, 200, 300, 500, even 800 strokes are administered. The foot swells up and then bursts open, and thus the blood spurts out. . . . On the next day, or, more exactly, during the night, as all ill-treatments are carried on at night . . . the whole bastinadoing is repeated again, in spite of the swollen feet and the wounds. . . . I was then in R., but in that prison there were . . . no less than thirty prisoners, who all had their feet in such a state that they began to burn and had to be amputated. . . . A young man was beaten to death within the space of five minutes."

These accounts from the Bryce-Toynbee report were selected more or less at random. At least, they are not notably more sensational than the hundred and fifty or so other statements in the book, the majority of which were "drawn from neutral witnesses who were living in or passing through Asiatic Turkey while these events were happening, and had opportunities of observing them."

THERE IS ALSO another voice from that period—that of Henry Morgenthau, United States Ambassador to Turkey during the early years of the World War, who published his recollections in 1918. From *Ambassador Morgenthau's*

Story: "In the early part of 1915, the Armenian soldiers in the Turkish army were reduced to a new status. Up to that time most of them had been combatants, but now they were all stripped of their arms and transformed into workmen . . . road laborers and pack animals. . . . They had to spend practically all their time in the open, sleeping on the bare ground. . . . They were given only scraps of food; if they fell sick they were left where they had dropped. . . .

"Let me relate a single episode which is contained in one of the reports of our consuls and which now forms part of the records of the American State Department. Early in July, 2,000 Armenian *amélés*—such is the Turkish word for soldiers who have been reduced to workmen—were sent from Harpoot to build roads. The Armenians in that town understood what this meant and pleaded with the Government for mercy. But this official insisted that the men were not to be harmed, and he even called upon the German missionary, Mr. Ehemann, to quiet the panic, giving that gentleman his word of honor that the ex-soldiers would be protected. . . . Yet practically every man of these 2,000 was massacred, and his body thrown into a cave. . . . A few days afterward another 2,000 soldiers were sent to Diyarbakir. The only purpose of sending these men out in the open country was that they might be massacred. In order that [they] might have no strength to resist . . . these poor creatures were systematically starved. Government agents went ahead on the road, notifying the Kurds that the caravan was approaching. . . . Not only did the Kurdish tribesmen pour down from the mountains upon this starved and weakened regiment, but the Kurdish women came with butcher's knives in order that they might gain that merit in Allah's eyes that comes from killing a Christian."

There is a photograph of Ambassador Morgenthau in the front of his book: a spare, elegant diplomat in his early sixties, with that look of nineteenth-century probity about him, and the same partly bald head and rimless eyeglasses one associates with his son, Henry Morgenthau, Jr., who was Secretary of the Treasury under President Franklin Roosevelt. The Ambassador's account continues:

"Yet these happenings did not constitute what the newspapers of the time commonly referred to as the Armenian atrocities; they were merely the preparatory steps in the destruction of the race. The Young Turks displayed greater ingenuity than their predecessor, Abdul-Hamid. . . . Instead of massacring outright the Armenian race, they now decided to deport it. In the south and southeastern section of the Ottoman empire lie the Syrian desert and Mesopotamian valley . . . a dreary, desolate waste, without cities and towns or life of any kind, populated only by a few wild and fanatical Bedouin tribes. . . . The Central Government now announced its intention of gathering the two million or more Armenians living in the several sections of the empire and transporting them to this desolate and inhospitable region."

FROM the Bryce-Toynbee report: "On the 8th April [1915] the final phase began, and the process . . . was applied to one Armenian centre after another throughout the Ottoman empire. On a certain date, in whatever town or village it might be (and the dates show a significant sequence), the public crier went through the streets announcing that every male Armenian must present himself forthwith at the Government Building. . . . The men presented themselves in their working clothes, leaving their shops and work-rooms open, their ploughs in the field, their cattle on the mountain side. When they arrived, they were thrown without explanation into prison, kept there a day or two, and then marched out of the town in batches, roped man to man, along some southerly or south-easterly road. They were starting, they were told, on a long journey—to Mosul or perhaps to Baghdad. . . . They had bidden no farewell to their families. . . . But they had not long to ponder over their plight, for they were halted and massacred at the first lonely place on the road. . . .

"After the Armenian men had been summoned away to their death, there was usually a few days' interval in whatever town it might be, and then the crier was heard again in the streets, bidding all Armenians who remained to prepare themselves for deportation, while placards to the same effect were posted on the walls. This applied, in actual fact, to the women and children, and to a poor remnant of the men who, through sickness, infirmity, or age, had escaped the fate marked out for their sex. . . .

"There was an official fiction that their banishment was only temporary, and they were therefore prohibited from selling their real property or their stock. The Government set its seal upon the vacated houses, lands, and merchandise, 'to keep them safe against their owners' return'; yet before these rightful owners started on their march they often saw these very possessions . . . made over by the authorities as a free gift to Muslim immigrants, who had been concentrated in the neighbourhood in readiness to step into the Armenians' place."

In some areas—for instance, in certain towns in the province of Bitlis—there was little pretense of deportation; most of the inhabitants were massacred instead.

From a *Statement by a German eyewitness . . . communicated by the American Committee for Armenian and Syrian Relief:* "In Harpoot and Mezré the people have had to endure terrible tortures. They have had their eyebrows plucked out, their breasts cut off, their nails torn off; their torturers hew off their feet or else hammer nails into them just as they do in shoeing horses. This is all done at nighttime, and in order that the people may not hear their screams and know of their agony, soldiers are stationed round the prisons, beating drums and blowing whistles. . . . Harpoot has become the cemetery of the Armenians."

The sufferings of the deportees were of a different order.

From a *Report by Fräulein M.* [a Swiss resident in Turkey], *dated 16th November, 1915:* "I have just returned from a ride on horseback through the Baghtché-Osmania plain, where thousands of exiles are lying out in the fields and on the roads, without any shelter and completely at the mercy of all manner of brigands. Last night about twelve o'clock, a little camp was suddenly attacked. There were about fifty to sixty persons in it. I found men and women badly wounded—bodies slashed open, broken skulls and terrible knife wounds. . . . In another camp we found thirty or forty thousand Armenians. I was able to distribute bread among them. Desperate and half-starved, they fell upon it. . . . I often saw them break down under their burden, but the soldiers kept on driving them forward with the butt-ends of their rifles, even sometimes with their bayonets. I have dressed bleeding wounds on the bodies of women that had been caused by these bayonet thrusts."

From a *Report by Fräulein O.* [another Swiss resident] *on a visit to the exiles' camp at Mamouret, 26th November, 1915:* "We saw thousands of tiny low tents, made of thin material. An innumerable crowd of people, of all ages . . . looking at us partly in surprise, partly with the indifference of desperation. A group of hungry, begging children and women were at our heels: '*Hanoum,* bread! *Hanoum,* I am hungry.' . . . Soon the immense procession was moving on. Some of the most miserable were left behind (others rested there already in the newly-dug graves)."

From a *Report by Fräulein M. on a visit to the exiles' camp at Islohia, 1st December, 1915:* "It had rained three days and three nights. . . . Many women had their feet frost-bitten; they were quite black and in a state for amputation. The wailing and groaning was horrible. . . . Though I had seen much distress before, the objects and the scenes I saw here defy description. A frailly-built woman was sitting by the roadside with her bedding on her back, and a young baby strapped on at the top of it, and in her arms she had a two-year-old child—its eyes were dim and it was at its last gasp. . . . The filth in and around these tents was something indescribable. On one single day the burial committee buried as many as 580 people."

The Berlin-Baghdad Railway, a joint German and Turkish enterprise, had been only partly completed, and the Anatolian portion ran from the suburbs of Constantinople southeast as far as Aleppo, on the edge of the Syrian desert. There were breaks in the line at both the Taurus and Amanus ranges. The use of the railroad to deport Armenians began in June 1915. The Armenians were packed into cattle cars and transported to the railheads, driven across the mountains on foot, and then taken by rail to Aleppo. Owing to a lack of engines and cattle cars, and the movement of troops up and down the small line, the Armenian deportees were frequently halted along the way and compelled to wait by the roadside for weeks, until new transportation could be found for them.

From a *Narrative of a journey . . . by a physician of foreign nationality, who had been resident in Turkey for ten years:* "At the first large station a sight burst upon my view which, although I knew and was prepared for it, was nevertheless a shock. There was a mob of a thousand or more people huddled about the station and environs, and long strings of cattle-trucks packed to suffocation with human beings. It was the first glimpse of the actual deportation of the Armenians. . . . There was no confusion, no wailing, no shouting, just a mob of subdued people, dejected, sad, hopeless, past tears. . . . At the station of K., as I looked across the fields to the river, I heard the Turkish commander say: 'Yes, I have 30,000 here under my charge.' Then I looked as far along the river as I could see, and it was one mass of improvised blanket tents."

From a *Letter, dated . . . 22nd November, 1915, from an American traveller:* "We began to pass one train after another, crowded, jammed with these poor people, being carried away. . . . At every station where we stopped, we came side by side with one of these trains. It was made up of cattle-trucks, and the faces of little children were looking out from behind the tiny barred windows of each truck. [At one station] the Armenians told us that they had been in the station for three days with no food. The Turks kept them from buying food. . . . One woman gave birth to twins in one of those crowded trucks, and crossing a river she threw both her babies and then herself into the water. . . . A German officer was on the train with us, and I asked him if Germany had anything to do with this deportation, for I thought it was the most brutal thing that had ever happened. He said: 'You can't object to exiling a race; it's only the way the Turks are doing it which is bad.' "

From a *Report from Dr. D., dated . . . 8th September,*

1915: "In P., the exiles are encamped in the open fields. . . . No protection is provided for them. . . . I have no knowledge of how many deaths have taken place. . . .

"The whip and club are in constant use by the police, and that upon women and children too. . . . A woman with a fractured thigh at the station was being helped by friends intending to bring her to the hospital. A commissary of police came along and ordered her to be dragged back into the carriage. . . . Soldiers' families are . . . said to be exempt from deportation, but in countless cases they are swept away with the rest. The men . . . are serving in the Turkish Army as loyally as any, and their families . . . are driven off in this inhuman manner."

From a *Letter from Dr. E., dated 27th October, 1915:* "Half a mile from the station I found two old women who were crawling about on hands and knees, too weak to walk; they had been carried off on a wagon, ostensibly to go to a village, but, once out of sight of the gendarmes, the driver had dropped them in a field and hurried away. . . . [They] looked forward to certain death by starvation, nor could we see any other future for them. A few miles farther on, we found a little heap of clods . . . and near it a bundle of rags full of a child's bones. The skull, with the scalp still clinging to it, was lying a yard or two away. Evidently there had been a hasty burial, and the dogs had come and torn the grave to pieces and devoured the body. That same day we found another dead body by the roadside—an old woman wrapped in a torn quilt; also a woman about forty years old sitting alone by the road, miles away from any city or village, with feet bare and swollen, almost pulseless, and evidently crazed from terror and exposure, muttering something about Turks who were coming to cut her throat, about her people who had left her behind. . . ."

WHILE the Armenians were thus being killed across Turkey in the middle months of 1915, either by massacre or by starvation, what of the great powers, notably England and France, whose attention the Armenian activists had so hoped to attract? These Allies, it seemed, had their hands full with the war. The Dardanelles campaign was at a standstill. Ambassador Morgenthau wrote: "When it at last became definitely established . . . that the traditional friends of Armenia—Great Britain, France, and Russia—could do nothing to help that suffering people, the mask began to disappear. In April I was suddenly deprived of the privilege of using the cipher for communicating with American consuls. The most rigorous censorship was applied to letters. Such measures could mean only that things were happening in Asia Minor which the authorities were determined to conceal."

In the spring and summer of 1915, at the height of the Armenian deportations, the two principal foreign presences in Constantinople were Morgenthau himself and Baron Hans von Wangenheim, the German Ambassador. Wangenheim, a career diplomat, regarded it as his main mission to keep Turkey in the war and so worked hard not to offend the Young Turk leaders. Generally, he passed on to Berlin without comment the Turkish government's prima-facie declarations that there was nothing much amiss in the Armenian provinces, that reports of massacres were exaggerations, and that such trouble as had occurred had been provoked by Armenian rebelliousness. When, in June, Talaat Pasha acknowledged to a German Embassy official that the mass deportations were not based alone on "military expediency" (as had previously been claimed), Wangenheim wrote to Berlin: "Talaat Bey has . . . openly stated that the Porte wished to take advantage of the opportunity offered by the war to make a clean sweep of their enemies at home without being troubled by foreign diplomatic intervention." On July 7, he pointed out again that the methods by which the Armenian deportations were being carried out "show that the Government is really aiming at the extermination of the Armenian race in the Ottoman empire." One of his stronger protests appears to have been a memorandum addressed to the grand vizier after the deportations had been in progress for nearly three months, in which he deplored the bad impression created abroad, and, in a kind of postscript, asked the Turks to watch out for "the manifold interests of German commerce and of the German welfare institutions in those provinces where the expulsion of Armenians is now being carried out."

Morgenthau in this period evidently felt different concerns, and conducted himself with less sense of diplomatic correctness—even with a certain largeness of spirit. "Two missionaries had just called upon me, giving the full details of the frightful happenings at Konia," he wrote. "After listening to their stories, I could not restrain myself, and went immediately to . . . Talaat. . . . I began to talk about the Armenians at Konia. I had hardly started when Talaat's attitude became . . . belligerent. His eyes lighted up, he brought his jaws together, leaned over toward me, and snapped out: 'Are *they* Americans?' In a moment Talaat said . . . 'The Armenians are not to be trusted. Besides, what we do with them does not concern the United States.'"

Morgenthau's *Story* continues: "I find in my diary on August 3d 'that Talaat is the one who desires to crush the poor Armenians.' He told me that the Union and Progress Committee had carefully considered the matter in all its details and that the policy which was being pursued was that which they had officially adopted. . . . 'Why are you so interested in the Armenians, anyway?' he said on another occasion. 'You are a Jew; these people are Christians. The Mohammedans and the Jews always get on harmoniously. We are treating the Jews here all right. What have you to complain of?'

"'You don't seem to realize,' I replied, 'that I am not here as a Jew but as American Ambassador. . . .'

"'We treat the Americans all right, too,' said Talaat. 'I don't see why you should complain.'"

Morgenthau had numerous meetings with the Young

Turk leaders—especially with Talaat, the Minister of the Interior, whom he regarded as having become the most powerful figure in the government: "I might as well have been talking to a stone wall. . . . 'These people,' he said, 'refused to disarm when we told them to. They opposed us at Van and at Zeitoun, and they helped the Russians. There is only one way in which we can defend ourselves against them in the future, and that is just to deport them.'

" 'Suppose a few Armenians did betray you,' I said. 'Is that a reason for destroying a whole race? Is that an excuse for making innocent women and children suffer?'

" 'Those things are inevitable,' Talaat replied. This remark to me was not quite so illuminating as one which Talaat made subsequently to a reporter of the *Berliner Tageblatt,* who asked him the same question: 'We have been reproached,' he said, according to this interviewer, 'for making no distinction between the innocent Armenians and the guilty; but that was utterly impossible, in view of the fact that those who were innocent today might be guilty tomorrow.' . . .

"I argued for a long time along these and similar lines. 'It is no use for you to argue,' Talaat answered. 'We have already disposed of three-quarters of the Armenians; there are none at all left in Bitlis, Van, and Erzurum. The hatred between the Turks and the Armenians is now so intense that we have got to finish with them. If we don't, they will plan their revenge.' . . .

"Talaat's attitude toward the Armenians was summed up

in the proud boast which he made to his friends: 'I have accomplished more toward solving the Armenian problem in three months than Abdul-Hamid accomplished in thirty years!' "

Morgenthau also attempted to put pressure on the Turks through the German Ambassador: "As soon as the early reports [of the massacres] reached Constantinople, it occurred to me that the most feasible way of stopping the outrages would be for the diplomatic representatives of all countries to make a joint appeal to the Ottoman Government.

"I approached Wangenheim on this subject in the latter part of March. His antipathy to the Armenians became immediately apparent. He began denouncing them in unmeasured terms. . . . 'The Armenians,' said Wangenheim, 'have shown themselves in this war to be enemies of the Turks. It is quite apparent that the two peoples can never live together in the same country. The Americans should move some of them to the United States, and we Germans will send some to Poland and in their place send Jewish Poles to the Armenian provinces—that is, if they will promise to drop their Zionist schemes.'

"Again, although I spoke with unusual earnestness, the Ambassador refused to help the Armenians. Still, on July 4th, Wangenheim did present a formal note of protest, but he did not talk to Talaat or Enver, the only men who had any authority, but to the grand vizier, who was merely a shadow. . . . [His protest's] only purpose was to put Germany officially on record. . . . Callous as Wangenheim showed himself to be, he was not quite so implacable toward the Armenians as the German naval attaché in Constantinople, Humann. . . .

"'I have lived in Turkey the larger part of my life,' he told me, 'and I know the Armenians. I also know that both Armenians and Turks cannot live together in this country. One of these races has got to go. And I don't blame the Turks for what they are doing to the Armenians. I think that they are entirely justified. The weaker nation must succumb.'"

THROUGH MOST OF 1915, the deportations continued. From a multitude of eyewitness reports, it is possible to determine that the first convoys started from the Armenian mountain town of Zeitoun, in Cilicia, on April 8, 1915 (almost two weeks before the allegedly provocative "rebellion" in Van), and thereafter steady streams of deportees were driven from the various Armenian centers of the Ottoman empire south toward the desert. According to the Bryce-Toynbee report, there is no record of any interruption or cessation of this mass movement until November 6, 1915: "On that date, an order from Constantinople reached the local authorities, at any rate in the Cilician plain, directing them to refrain from further deportations; but this applied only to the remnant of the local Armenian residents, and the masses of exiles from the north and the northwest who were still painfully struggling across the barriers of Taurus and Amanus were driven on remorselessly to their journey's end." This was either along the wayside or, finally, in the dry and barren deserts of the south, where—for example, outside the desolate and malarial village of Der-el-Zor, which was virtually uninhabited—an evolving twentieth-century institution (borrowed from the Spanish practices of 1896 in Cuba as well as from the British in the Boer War) made its appearance: the concentration camp.

In the first phase of the over-all process, Armenian men had been drafted into the Turkish Army, then disarmed in the labor battalions and massacred, and the men who remained in the towns and villages had also been disarmed, sometimes imprisoned and tortured, and then either killed by the gendarmes or marched out to be massacred by the Kurds. In the second phase, the remainder of the Armenian population, which meant mostly women and children and older men, had been either packed in cattle cars on the Berlin-Baghdad Railway or driven south on foot across the mountains.

From the Bryce-Toynbee report: "From the moment they left the outskirts of the towns, they [the deportees] were never safe from outrage. The Muslim peasants mobbed and plundered them as they passed through the cultivated lands, and the gendarmes [in charge of the convoys] connived at the peasants' brutality. . . . When they arrived at a village they were exhibited like slaves in a public place . . . and every Muslim inhabitant was allowed to view them and take his choice of them. . . . The gendarmes themselves began to make free with the rest. . . .

"There were still more horrible outrages when they came to the mountains, for here they were met by bands of 'chettis' and Kurds. The 'chettis' were brigands recruited from the public prisons. . . . When these Kurds and 'chettis' waylaid the convoys, the gendarmes always fraternised with them and followed their lead. . . .

"It depended on the whim of the moment whether a Kurd cut a woman down or carried her away into the hills. . . . But while the convoy dwindled, the remnant had always to march on. The cruelty of the gendarmes towards the victims grew greater as their physical sufferings grew more intense. . . . The passage of rivers, and especially of the Euphrates, was always an occasion of wholesale murder. Women and children were driven into the water, and were shot as they struggled. . . .

"The last survivors often straggled into Aleppo naked. . . . [Others] were transported to Aleppo by rail. . . . At Bozanti, the railhead west of Taurus, and again at Osmania, Mamouret, Islohia, and Kotma . . . vast and incredibly foul concentration camps grew up, where the exiles were delayed for months, and died literally by thousands of hunger, exposure, and epidemics."

The third phase began with that remnant of the Armenians which reached Aleppo, for Aleppo was the point upon which all convoys converged, and those few who had survived the deportations that far were soon marched off again, southeast, into the Syrian desert.

From *Armenia and the Near East,* by Fridtjof Nansen, High Commissioner for Refugees under the League of Nations, published in 1928: "At Meskne on the Euphrates, east of Aleppo, where the Armenians were starved to death in one of the great concentration camps, 55,000 people, according to Turkish figures, lie buried. It is estimated that during 1915, 60,000 deportees were sent to Der-el-Zor on the Euphrates; and the majority of them disappeared. On April 15, 1916, 19,000 were sent in four batches to Mosul, three hundred kilometres across the desert; but only 2,500 arrived. . . . Some of the women and girls had been sold to Bedouins on the way; the rest had died of hunger and thirst. In July, 1916, 20,000 were deported to Der-el-Zor; eight weeks later, according to the testimony of a German officer, only a few artisans were left."

In 1912, the Armenian patriarchate in Constantinople had estimated the Armenian population in Turkey at two million one hundred thousand. This was considered a fairly high figure, since the patriarchate traditionally inflated its membership rolls. After the war, the Turks retroactively released their own pre-deportation figures, which placed the Armenians at one million one hundred thousand—an implausibly low figure. According to the several religious and relief agencies that looked into the situation, the most likely total for the number of Armenians in Turkey before the war fell somewhere between the two statistics. Thus, the American Committee for Armenian and Syrian Relief in 1916 estimated the prewar Armenian population of Turkish Armenia at a million eight hundred thousand. Statistics from 1916 show that there were about a hundred and fifty thousand Armenians in Constantinople and Smyrna who, owing mainly to their visibility, were not subjected to deportation; approximately a hundred and eighty-five thousand Armenians, mostly from the province of Van, who accompanied an invading Russian force when it withdrew to the Russian Caucasus in 1915; approximately eight hundred thousand Armenians, the majority of them in clearly moribund condition, who were uncovered by relief agencies in the concentration camps of the desert and elsewhere across Turkey.

Thus, it is possible to say, not precisely but with a general respect for accuracy and plausibility, that in the course of the 1915–16 massacres and deportations close to one million Armenians—more than half the Armenian population of Turkey—disappeared; which is to say, were killed, outright by police or soldiers, or by roadside massacres, or by forced marches, or by starvation, or by sickness, or by conditions in the concentration camps.

On August 31, 1915, Talaat Pasha declared to his German allies, *"La question Arménienne n'existe plus."*

What was one to make of such a story? I use the word "make" in the sense of "to fashion or create"; or perhaps, in this instance, "to re-create," for there was no point in claiming either that nothing—no myth or dream—had been made of the Armenian story up to now or that what had been made had been in any way useful to the Armenians or to the world. For could one say that self-pity had been useful? Had anger been helpful or creative—this special anger of the Armenians, sometimes wild and childlike, as in the case of men such as Sarkis, for whom the Turks (turned into devils by one set of myths) had been stuck in the Armenian belly like a lump of hot coal; and sometimes an anger ingrown and self-deceiving, as I supposed was felt by men such as my father, for whom the slaying of their forebears (perhaps Christified by the same set of myths) represented such pain and mortification that they could never turn their faces to it?

On the other hand, was it in the end possible for any citizen of the twentieth century—this century of genocide, and bloodshed, and napalm-bombing, and police interrogation—to find some particular meaning in one example of political terror and mass murder as opposed to other examples of political terror and mass murder; in one instance of genocide as opposed to other (smaller? larger?) instances of genocide? Was it not perhaps, finally, more to the point, more useful, to adopt the realism of the era one lived in, and to say, with the grave modesty of someone who has discovered a major truth at no pain to himself: Such is life. Such surely are the facts of life and the human condition— of the universal context of pain and misery. Has there not always been torture and mass murder?

It was easy for the soul to cry "No" to any quick agreement with this view, for souls—certainly souls on American diets—are notoriously hopeful and idealistic, ready to identify with the optimistic affirmation of the Ascension, reluctant to fasten much attention on the process of the Crucifixion. But in this matter one's reason also answered "No." For, although there were certain exceptions, certain obscurities and dark passages in history which precluded one's making a universal law on the subject, nonetheless it seemed generally untrue that life had been precisely, or even approximately, "such," or that there had "always" been such torture and killing. At least, in this one respect it was untrue: in the scale and deliberateness of the killing.

Serious students of the epidemiology of modern violence, such as Hannah Arendt, have written amply and cogently on the increase in mass violence which has taken place in the twentieth century as the energies of technocracy and of the technocratic mind have been added to man's ancient propensity for aggression and murder. It was banality, Dr.

Arendt noted—the methodology of an advanced bureaucracy—that made possible the extent of the slaughter of the
Jews in Germany, and not necessarily some spurt in man-
kind's inherent wickedness.

There is reason to believe that this harnessing of modern
technology to political mass murder began with the instance
of the Turks and the Armenians. Or, if it did not actually
begin on such-and-such a date, at such-and-such a place (for
one should be wary of asserting such "firsts"), then one can
say at least that the Turkish massacres and "deportations" of
the Armenians were the most notable early example of the
employment of modern communications and technology in
the acting out and realization of political violence.

For, clearly, the entire production—or orchestration, if
one will—of the Armenian genocide was based on the im-
perfectly utilized but definitely perceived capacities of the
modern state for politically restructuring itself, which were
made possible by the engines of technology. In due course, to
be sure, Hitler's Germany was to perfect the process of railway deportation and to develop the gas chamber and the
crematoria, and Lenin's and Stalin's Russia was to evolve
further the institutions of the concentration camp and secret
surveillance—as most modern nations now, in scientific concert, have advanced the techniques of efficiently administered torture by the use of electric current. But in virtually
every modern instance of mass murder, beginning, it appears, with the Armenians, the key element—not the only
element but the key element, which has raised the numerical

and psychic levels of the deed above the classic terms of massacre—has been the alliance of technology and communications: interior communications, such as permit concerted action on the part of a government and its agents, enabling the "net" to be widely cast and the casting of it to be part of a unified procedure; and what is by no means the lesser system of exterior communications, whereby the facts about these objects of government action (these "victims," or "rebels," or "freedom fighters," or "anarchists") are communicated to witness-populations, although they have usually been transformed to the convenience of the government that controls the system. This transformation has the effect of disconnecting the victims from the rest of the world, and even from their own people.

Was the Armenian story, then, a fable of communications, a parable of the failure of language? At this stage, one might acknowledge the obvious: that it was a story composed of a multitude of parts. It was a story of unresolved hostility (the Turks) and of a prolonged national psychic depression (the Armenians); a story of misconceived brotherhood (the Turks and the Armenians) and of bravery and pain and the reduction of personality through terror; a story, also, at least by indirection, of the moral ambitions and ambiguities of the great European Christian democracies; and, not insignificantly, a story, running as a generality—indeed, one might call it a bloody river linking the great murderous events of our century—of the intrinsic weakness, perhaps a weakness identical with that of human nature itself, of the modern system of communications, in which in recent eras virtually all nations have at some crucial point acquiesced.

Acquiescence. What if the witness-clients of the worldwide communications systems had not acquiesced in 1915 and 1916, when letters from schoolteachers and missionaries first began appearing in the Zurich and Basel papers? It is a question impossible to answer, and perhaps pointless, ignoring, as it does, the profound unseriousness of human beings everywhere, and their insistently parochial concerns. What if? Would the English and the French have returned to the Dardanelles? Would a Crusade of Zurich schoolteachers have departed for the Golden Horn? What if? Perhaps one might say that it had been a challenge to a small, unreliable element of the human spirit—a challenge that was never taken up, that was put forward again later, and again, and again, and again, and has still not been taken up. According to documents presented at the Nuremberg trials in 1945, Adolf Hitler, in a discussion with Hermann Goering about the imminent invasion of Poland, asked, "Who still talks nowadays of the extermination of the Armenians?" It was another question without an answer.

BUT IF IT WAS POSSIBLE, and perhaps necessary in a rationalistic sense, to view the Armenian genocide from a political level, even from the rather cool perspective of a student of technology and communications, maybe this was something of a luxury for an Armenian—even a part-Armenian, like me. Somehow it begged the question. For the question was: What—beyond the journalistic facts—had happened to the Armenians? All along, in my search for Armenia and the Armenian ethos, I had found that Armenians—in their books or in their statements, in their cups or sometimes matter-of-factly on the street—always came back to this matter of the "massacres," of the "genocide." It would have been cruel or trivial to align this refrain with the standard simile of the broken record: the sounds of a needle that would not, could not, lift itself out of a particular, twisted groove. One knew that this fixation came from something deep, as deep as trauma. One knew that the question (What had really happened?) was not answerable entirely in terms of history or politics, or even of technology or communications, of fixing blame on this side or that side. In the end, one guessed, it was not even answerable mainly in terms of how many had been killed, as if the sheer numerical dimensions of the act (a million dead!) might somehow explain the particular condition of the survivors. This last was not an irrelevant statistic, but it referred backward more than forward, more to the dead than to the living. One hoped that if the question was to be answered at all, it was to be answered for the living.

Ever since I began this journey to Armenia, my father's presence had hovered near me, by no means always approvingly. I had seen his face in dreams and in museums, and had come to find that natural. He was my father. I felt a presence—no, more than that, an invocation—of fathers everywhere around me. What had Sarkis said that afternoon, almost in pain? "Your father was an Armenian. You must respect him." It lingered in my mind. Fathers and sons. Phrases echoed in my head: "My father had committed no crime." And "We were innocent, we were helpless."

A picture began to form of yet other fathers and other sons. I thought of all the Armenian fathers who had been drafted into the Turkish Army in that year of 1914: men who were fathers, in dun-colored uniforms, shipped away from their towns and later killed; fathers sent to prison or else massacred along a roadside. How many Armenian children had seen their fathers killed? Or—worse, perhaps—had watched their mothers and sisters brutalized to death, or close to death, in their fathers' absence? In that one traumatic period, how many Armenian sons had felt betrayed by their fathers' absence—for what do children comprehend of reasons and explanations, what does a child understand in his soul of a father's nonappearance in a time of need?

Abraham, the father, threatened his son Isaac with a knife stroke—an act of demonic or holy passion, a massacre. Jesus was killed out of hate, but first He was brutalized with the torture of crucifixion. And then the Son called to his Father: "My God, my God, why hast thou forsaken me?"

Betrayal breeds hatred, but how does a son hate his father? How does a son knowingly hate a father who sired him, protected him, and only then (and for the rest of the son's life) abandoned him as the result of his own murder?

Or knowingly hate a mother whom he has been compelled to watch being reduced to a subhuman level?

The Turks, yes. It was possible for an Armenian to hate the Turks. But here one noticed something interesting. For the Turks had never accepted this hate. Unlike the Germans after the Second World War, who had (albeit with difficulty and disclaimers) acknowledged the fact of war crimes and war guilt toward the Jews, who had even fashioned grisly shrines out of Dachau and Buchenwald and had held trials of their own, the Turks had made no official admission of guilt or criminality toward the Armenians.

Where else might the hatred go?

Toward the self: self-hatred. One hesitated to advance so simple an explanation of such a complicated subject; still, that was what it seemed to come down to. One thought of the wailing or hand-wringing quality of many Armenians— especially the older men, but also the sons—whose physical gestures seemed directed more against themselves than against the alleged object, the Turks. The diatribes against the Turks—tantrums, as it were, carried down now through three generations. Wasn't the surest way of tormenting an angry child as follows: to leave it alone, ignored in its rage?

Self-hatred. "We were innocent, we were helpless." The fact that had emerged from a study of the Armenians in Turkey at the beginning of the First World War was that they had been neither entirely innocent nor altogether help-less. Where there had been any possibility of resistance—at Van, at Zeitoun, at the small settlement of Mousa Dagh, which had been near enough to the Mediterranean coast for a French warship to intercede briefly—the Armenians had fought with skill and courage. Nor had the guerrilla operations of the Armenian Volunteers been on the level of prankish afternoon escapades of Constantinople rug merchants. The majority of the Armenians in Turkey, one realized, had been put on the defensive not so much by actual disarmament (that had been the final stroke) as by the cumulative years of mental and social depression which had led to the disarmament—disarmament at the hands of their brothers the Turks.

Did not suicide studies of various European nations in the Second World War reveal that in periods of resistance, or of the greatest danger, the suicide rate fell? In periods when resistance dwindled, when the enemy occupation became more entrenched, men again began to kill themselves —the ultimate act of self-hatred. After five hundred years of living as *"giaours"* or *"raya"* in a Muslim society, the kings of Nairi had been gradually changed into the likeness of Artin, the inn clerk. And these Artins had one day looked in their mirrors and detested what they saw.

For the first time in my life, I thought I saw my father clearly. Some little while ago, I had seen how his face, with its coolness and authority, its supposed impassivity, concealed within it the silent, helpless fury of that man in the blue velvet hat. But it had taken me this long to understand where the fury had been directed: at himself, Dikran Kouyoumjian. I thought, This proud and sensitive man—how he must have hated growing up an Armenian in England, not so much because of being condescended to by the English (although there was bound to have been that) as because of being himself marked, or feeling marked, by the collective guilt and self-hatred proceeding from a race that had been hated unto death. For that was the curse of genocide: death took the victims, but over the survivors settled a mark, a "fallout," of having been hated unto death.

I thought of the struggle, all the wriggles, he had made throughout his life to avoid being Armenian, to escape from this "collective unconscious." His detached manner. The mask of not caring about, not bothering about, his racial past. Not even writing about it—the "it," after all, being his identity, the one solid piece of wood that any writer has.

I wondered how many Armenian sons had felt abandoned by their fathers: abandoned into nothing more than their Armenianness, that racial psyche of guilt, of anger without an object and always disguised as something else— braggadocio or saturnine lament, darkness or light. Such a *waste,* it seemed. I thought, If only he could have told me about this! Then what? What would I have done? I realized I would have done nothing, except be more afraid. Besides, he hadn't known it himself.

And so one afternoon, with the sun pale and glowing in the gray-blue sky, my wife and I drove out once again with Sarkis in the borrowed limousine toward the plain of Ararat. It was our last expedition, although none of us had said so. Sarkis sat behind the wheel of the car, driving quite slowly—or so it seemed—past fields that were now yellow everywhere, fields of rock and yellow grass. Once, we stood in line for perhaps fifteen minutes behind three bullock carts, which gave Sarkis occasion to display his patience and to discourse on the necessary mechanization of rural life. Back in the hotel, our suitcases had already been lifted down from the top of the tall cherry-wood armoire and were waiting to be filled.

It had been my idea that we should drive out in this direction for a final look at Ararat. Sarkis had said that there was a little village along the way which we should examine—or perhaps it was a church within a village. My wife sat close beside me and held my hand. I knew she was genuinely sorry to leave. "I remember this road so well," she said at one point. I thought, Yes, I remember it, too, but differently—as if I had been different when I last went down it. For it was the road to the Monument, which we had visited on our first day in Erevan: the Monument on the plain of Ararat. Had Sarkis known that I wished us to go there again? Had I wished us to go there again? I thought the answer to both questions was yes.

Sarkis blinked in the glare of the sun. He seemed uncommonly vulnerable then: a creature blinking.

"Would you like my sunglasses?" I said.

Sarkis shook his head. "No, thank you. I must train my eyes."

In front of us, perhaps a mile away, some red buses were parked.

"See, we are at the Monument," said Sarkis.

"Let's stop here," I said.

"If you wish," said Sarkis.

I felt a nearly unbearable closeness to Sarkis just then, so that I wanted to touch him. No, it was more than that: an intimacy. But what is intimacy? I was intimate with my wife, but I wished to embrace Sarkis. As I looked at him, I could see the pores of his face sweating—this alien face that I wished to embrace. I could feel my wife's hand tighten its grip on mine.

Sarkis parked our car beside the red buses, and we walked up the incline and then out across the open field toward the familiar structure of angled columns, slanting together, in the mid-distance, almost like an incomplete metal tepee. Sarkis walked ahead of us. To the right of us—a moving, shifting cluster of white shirts and bare legs—a group of schoolchildren formed a circle of their own in the field. Were they standing? Listening? Their voices, like the cries of tropical birds, floated across the silence. In the far distance, Ararat (that primeval monument) rose from the open plain. Again I thought, We are in the middle of nowhere.

The snow gleamed white around the peak of Ararat. Ararat . . . Urartu. What a noble fantasy it was to have conceived of waves lapping beneath the peak of Ararat. I thought suddenly of Viscount Bryce, who, in the eighteen-seventies, at the age of thirty-eight, had climbed to the summit. Afterward, two members of his expedition reported that they had found several pieces of wood—"possibly driftwood, for which there was no logical explanation, owing to the barrenness of the summit." Bryce, however, had refrained from stating that the wood had been left over from the Ark. "A spectacular view is afforded from just below the main peak of Ararat," he wrote, "and in every respect it is a most inspiring and exhilarating climb; although if it was here that Noah rested his Ark we shall have need of further proof." A measured man, Viscount Bryce—not one to jump to hasty conclusions about driftwood on mountain peaks.

I heard Sarkis's voice in front of me, talking once more to my wife about the Monument: "Each time I come here, I marvel at the ingenuity of our Armenian architects. Look how these great slabs lie at an angle without support! See for yourself—there is nothing holding them up."

I thought, How strange to finally meet one's past: to simply meet it, the way one might finally acknowledge a person who had been in one's company a long while. So, it's you!

I was standing by myself beneath the overhanging slabs of the Monument, looking into the fire. I remember thinking that if I had had a flower in my hand I would gladly have thrown it into the fire, but that I hadn't remembered to pick one. My eyes went out to the open fields beyond the fire, the fields of yellow flowers. I thought that it didn't matter about the flower; I thought suddenly that I was home. It was the flattest, simplest, lightest of feelings. I thought, So this is what it's all about.

And then I felt my father's hand in mine. It was so strong a feeling that today I can almost (but not quite) recover that imaginary touch. But what I responded to was not merely the "touch"—I had felt that before, at many moments in my life. One of the key memories of my childhood had been a nearly tactile recollection of being pulled by the hand (were we running? walking?) by my father down an unremembered street—an unremembered time except for the pull of the hand, even his face out of sight, his expression unknown, only his arm extending from a dark overcoat.

But I knew that this time it was different, and as I stood there I knew that it would always afterward be different (as it has been). For the hand I felt was not pulling me; it was the hand of a man which I had briefly held in my own one afternoon in New York, the hand of my father dying. His hand had been so frail in mine that afternoon, so frail, and even small—smaller than mine—and I remember how the feel of this hand had been such a shock to me then (more than his fading speech, or pale features, or struggle of recognition): this hand of my father, who was releasing me, releasing himself from me, and me from him (as if either thing were possible between fathers and sons). And I had not known how to grip him back. But here his hand was again. I felt that I held it in mine. I felt that somehow I had brought him here—to this place. I didn't know what else I felt or knew, but I wept, large tears streaming down my face. I wasn't even sure for what. Nor did it feel bad. On the contrary, it felt quite natural.

"I knew that you would be overcome before you left," said Sarkis, who had come up beside me. I could see my wife looking at me, at the tears that were on my cheeks. Sarkis clasped me by the shoulder. "No Armenian can stand here," he said, "and not be moved by the suffering of the Armenian people."

I could feel Sarkis's arms around me, his warm bulk against mine. I thought, Kinsman, brother . . . so be it. I thought, We Armenians sweat a lot.

"Did you bring flowers?" I asked.

"Of course," said Sarkis.

My wife and I each took a yellow flower from his hands and tossed it into the fire, which consumed the flowers in its orange flame.

The three of us walked together, slowly, away from the Monument, along the narrow path that led across the yellow fields. The schoolchildren seemed to be playing far in the distance, arms and legs moving, their voices unheard. My wife had her arm in mine. Sarkis was talking of the last year his father had been alive, when he and his brothers carried the old man onto the plain of Ararat and the old man spent the afternoon asleep in the field.

I wondered if in early spring the whole valley was filled with flowers. I wondered if the snow at the top of Ararat ever melted. It seemed hard to comprehend that there should always be so much life and death side by side. I thought that, although I could never explain it, it was true that I had somehow brought my father here. I thought, How long and circuitous the voyage has been that brought all of us here—Armenians forever nearly sailing off the edge of the earth.

And then we left: one morning, early, with the sun slowly rising above the rim of the olive-green hills.

The hotel porters were scrubbing the well-worn floor of the lobby as if one of the archangels were shortly to arrive. Such seamen's labor! Vartan appeared to bid us goodbye. His mood was even more matter-of-fact than usual, but one guessed that he had arisen an hour or so earlier than he normally did, and was making his clarity of vision a present to us. He asked if we had heard that the Armenian soccer team had just achieved first place in the Soviet Union.

No, we hadn't—although, now that I thought of it, there had been much shouting late the previous night down the hotel corridor where the television set was kept.

"Yes," said Vartan solemnly. "Last evening, we defeated the Ukraine. Now we are No. 1." He could hardly suppress his pleasure, and I wished we might exchange cigars or all rush off to a crowded tavern and have several drinks, for in my present mood it seemed indeed a wonderful piece of news—a fortuitous piece of news. Somehow it answered well: the Ararat team was No. 1.

"Of course, they won't stay up there," said Vartan. "They play Moscow next weekend."

Of course. We shook hands with Vartan, shyly, like parents leaving a boy at school. Vartan seemed to become younger with each moment that the short ceremony extended. Finally, he clutched his briefcase, almost waved it as a talisman against the leave-taking process. "Have good luck in your journey!" he called.

"I hope you stay No. 1," I said inanely.

Vartan grinned like the Cheshire Cat and vanished.

SARKIS TOOK US out to the airport. He wore the familiar brown suit and clutched two packages: a book and a colored calendar he had bought for us—in return, perhaps, for some all too inconsequential gifts we had presented to him the day before. There was an exchange of addresses, with that formality which comes upon people who have been unexpectedly close and are now parting. I kept wanting to say, "Something important has happened to me here." But it seemed too imprecise—and also too important—to speak about on that basis. I talked instead of the "good times" we had had—the interestingness of the visit, and so on. The streets and pink stone apartment houses of Erevan sped by outside the car window. There were suddenly so many things I wanted to say to Sarkis, for I had found out in my soul that we were both Armenian, which I knew in a certain sense was neither here nor there but in another sense was nearly everything; and now he was staying here in this hard and unsafe place, and I was going home—to another home—sailing softly in my soft boat to my calm American harbor, where "starvation" and "disease" were words one read in newspapers, and "murder" was what one watched on television, and "massacre" was a synonym for what happened in athletic contests. Clearly, I was no different from my countrymen. On the other hand, I had found out that I had many different countrymen.

"Look!" said Sarkis, pointing to a somber brick office building under construction. "We are always working."

"Sarkis, it's a fine place here," I said.

"I knew you'd be proud of it," he said.

It was true. I was proud.

IN THE AIRPORT, a different reality intervened. Our Aeroflot plane was bound for Beirut, where we were to change for a flight to Istanbul, and then New York. Now, in the little Erevan airport, which decidedly had the air about it of a Balkan border crossing in wartime, well-armed soldiers in gray uniforms and Armenian passengers, mostly in peasant costumes, mingled with one another, body pressing against body in the crowded chamber, all somehow bound together in the modern police ritual of Search and Examination. Everywhere on the gray concrete floor the suitcases of these passengers had been flung open. Articles of clothing were scattered as in cartoons of department-store bargain sales. The Armenian peasants scrambled about on the floor picking things up, stuffing them back, taking more out. The soldier policemen walked about in the disorder. They, too, were Armenians.

A young man stood next to us in line—by no means a peasant, either, but wearing a proper dark-blue business suit, and clutching two suitcases, a couple of enormous and grotesque dolls, a paper bag filled with pastries, and a large giftshop oil painting of a sunset, the sun setting over Lake Sevan. After spilling out the contents of his suitcases, the soldiers produced knives and slashed open the fabric lining at the top and bottom of each one. The young man was compelled to pry off the heads of the two dolls he was carrying; having done that, and now holding the two heads in his arms, he pushed the painting toward a soldier, who took his knife and proceeded to remove the picture from its frame, and the canvas from the cardboard backing.

When we reached the inspection point, our American passports were produced and briefly examined, and (surprising to someone who grew up with the drama and myth of the Cold War) we were let by without any search. Except for our book satchel, which weighed an unusual amount and was opened. Books on the Crusades and Abdul-Hamid and the Turkish massacres were blandly riffled through and returned. Two volumes remained on the counter: *A History of Russia,* by Sir Bernard Pares, and *Twenty Letters to a Friend,* by Stalin's daughter, which my wife had been reading, and which now stared up at us— burglar tools uncovered in the trunk of our car. A stern young Russian officer came along and picked up the books.

"We will hold these," he said. I nodded agreeably, quite icy with tension.

Behind us lay the litter of clothes upon the floor. The young Armenian with the two doll heads was trying to join his picture frame back together—a fairly hopeless task. An old woman bent over several empty suitcases, stuffing all sorts of clothing back in. It was a miserable sight, a miserable and hateful process, and there seemed to be something evil in our having been even partly exempt from it: power politics once again working their will upon common humanity. Sir Bernard Pares and Svetlana Alliluyeva had been slight hostages to fortune compared to that knocked-about sun setting over Lake Sevan.

As WE WALKED out toward the airplane, we could see Sarkis standing in a knot of people just outside the airport building. There were gray-uniformed soldiers in front of the small crowd. Sarkis waved and called out something, which was lost in the noise of the plane engines. We waved back, and kept walking—across the runway and up the steps of the aircraft. The noise of the engines was very loud. The snow on Ararat gleamed in the distance. Sarkis still waved, his small, stocky, brown-suited figure planted beside the small stone building, waving, a hand waving. Going, gone.

Our leave-taking had seemed oddly abrupt and disjointed, but perhaps it was truer to life that way, or, at least, truer to itself.

In the plane, my wife asked me, "Are you sad to leave?" "No," I replied.

I had embraced this stranger, Sarkis, as my kinsman, and had felt it, or had thought I felt it; and had come to comprehend things about my father that I had not known before; and had seen churches and refrigerator factories; and had heard Armenian spoken at breakfast, lunch, and dinner. And now it was time to get back.

My wife said, "How do you suppose the story ends?"

The Armenian story? Far below us now, and swiftly receding, could be seen the outline of Erevan: smoke rising from one or two factories; the buildings pressed together as if in a large village. Of course, it was more than a large village; the soccer team was No. 1. I thought, Perhaps if the Armenians have a good enough soccer team they will forget the wretched Turks.

We were flying toward Ararat now, its peak nearly level with our airplane, perhaps ten miles away. It seemed exciting that we would pass so close to Ararat. Then, suddenly, we banked—a steep bank that clattered some loose objects in the rear of the cabin. Somebody behind us said something with the word "Turkish." Of course, we were avoiding the Turkish border. Turkish air space—what an odd concept! Ararat, with its driftwood and radar.

"Where are we heading?" my wife asked.

"I think east toward Azerbaijan and then south."

OUR AIRPLANE sped high above the dark-green ridges of the Caucasus. Below, there seemed to be nothing except trees and rock outcroppings and, here and there, the slender brown line of a country road. From this perspective, the region appeared utterly wild and empty of all life. And Armenia, one realized, was so small that by then we had almost surely passed beyond it—a tiny island in the ocean of the Soviet Union. It was impossible not to think that here was a difficult place for the Armenians to have ended up— squeezed into this rock-strewn, harshly beautiful, relatively infertile northern sector of the old Urartian perimeter, as subject-citizens of yet another great autocratic empire. On the other hand, I remembered something that Sarkis had said one afternoon as we tramped around the ruins of an ancient Armenian church—the remains of walls and cornices tumbled, as usual, about the ground by unnamed invaders, or pillagers, or natural forces. "Tell me, my friends, where are the Lydians and Phrygians today?" he called cheerfully, standing on an overturned slab of basalt. "Where are the mighty Assyrians and the Cappadocians?" In some ways, doubtless, history was like a game of musical chairs, although it was hard to tell whether the Lydians, Phrygians, etc., had sat down too early or too late. But I also remembered what Sarkis had said, in a different mood, only the evening before, when, as we walked across the square, I asked him if his colleague Kevork had received any news yet about his son. Sarkis had shaken his head. Then, pointing to Lenin's statue ahead of us, which seemed suddenly obtrusive in the gray twilight, he had said simply, almost casually, "Try to understand, we have many necessary modern advantages this way. You might say it is a bargain that Armenians have made with the world—perhaps not always knowing we were making it."

Probably that was so, I thought—although when I remembered the scene at the airport it seemed a heavy dosage of reality for radish-growers, distinguished astronomers, soccer players, and even bargainers to live with. In any event, Armenians had certainly not reached their present geographical or political situation as a result of any *Armenian* grand design. Stated simply, what had happened was this. A large number of the survivors of the Young Turk massacres—roughly a hundred and eighty-five thousand of them—fled north to the protection of the Russian Caucasus. There they joined with the Russian Armenians in the Transcaucasian provinces, chiefly in Tiflis, Erevan, Elizavetpol, and Kars, to form a scattered Armenian population of around two million. For much of the previous century, the czarist government had expressed at least a public concern for the Armenians in Turkey, and at the beginning of the war it had declared a willingness to grant autonomy to the territories of the Turkish Armenians. By mid-1916, Russian troops had advanced well into the now nearly desolate provinces of Turkish Armenia, reaching a line as far west as Trebizond and as far south as Bitlis. Then, having benefited militarily from the help of the Armenian Volunteers, the czarist government dissolved them, and it became clear that Russia intended to annex rather than liberate Turkish Armenia.

But early in 1917 the Romanovs were overthrown. Under the new Provisional Russian government, the provinces of Turkish Armenia were given a civil administration, with many posts being filled by Armenians. Refugees began returning to Erzurum, Van, and Bitlis. However, in the fall, when the Bolsheviks took power, the tide turned once more. Lenin wanted to take his new government out of the war, and Russian forces everywhere began to fall back. In March 1918, Lenin signed the Treaty of Brest-Litovsk with the Central Powers and Turkey, which, among other things, permitted the Turks not only to regain the Turkish-Armenian provinces but also to reoccupy three northern Armenian districts that the Russians had taken in 1877. As the Russian troops withdrew from the Turkish front, with Russian soldiers heading homeward in thousands, a Turkish army corps marched north again, pushing well into the Caucasus, and by early April of 1918 had moved almost to the old prewar boundaries.

Centuries of powerlessness under the Turks and years of political anti-establishment activities in czarist Russia and the Ottoman empire had not produced a very sizable cadre of Armenian governing experts and administrators. Even so, in May of 1918, while the Turkish army corps continued to push northward, the Armenians concentrated themselves in the province of Erevan and announced the formation of an independent republic—as did the Georgians to the northwest, and the Muslim Azerbaijanis to the east. Starvation was widespread in the Caucasus then, because grain shipments by railroad from the Ukraine had ceased, and it was perhaps especially harsh in the less fertile areas of the new Republic of Armenia. To make matters worse, the Armenians, now virtually alone in their battle against the Turks, had also to fight the Azerbaijanis, who had formed an alliance with their fellow Muslims. Clearly, it was not a propitious time or place for the founding of small independent states. Some of the alternatives were not especially appealing, however; for instance, when a combined Turkish and Azerbaijani force captured Baku—then a Bolshevik-Armenian enclave in Azerbaijani territory—General Halil Pasha tactfully kept his Ottoman units from entering the city for twenty-four hours, while the Azerbaijani troops and the citizenry massacred the fifteen or twenty thousand Armenians who had remained behind.

Still, when the First World War ended, in the autumn of 1918, the Turks were compelled to relinquish Baku and to fall back from their recent advance. The Armenians believed that their time had finally arrived. An Allied fleet steamed into the Bosporus and anchored off Constantinople. The incumbent sultan, Muhammad VI, was in effect an Allied puppet, willing to accept Turkey's partition if he could hang on to whatever was left. When the European powers began assembling in Paris for the peace conference, the Republic of Armenia dispatched emissaries from Erevan to Paris, where, joining with a delegation of émigré Turkish Armenians, they sought to persuade the Allied delegates to create—from the expected dissolution of the Ottoman empire—an independent Armenian state that would include not only the provinces of the Armenian plateau but also Cilicia, and would receive protection from the Turks by being mandated to one of the great powers.

But even as the Armenians lobbied in Paris for their new nation—spreading out their maps before President Woodrow Wilson, who on several occasions had expressed himself in favor of an autonomous Armenia stretching from the Caucasus to the Mediterranean—the situation changed again. For the victorious Allies had overplayed their hand in parceling out defeated Turkey to the British, the French, the Italians, and the Greeks, with the result that an intense new Turkish nationalism had been aroused, personified by the "hero of Gallipoli," Mustafa Kemal. While the delegates in Paris and, later, in San Remo deliberated on their reapportionment of the Ottoman empire, Lenin, in Moscow, and Kemal, who had raised a rebel army in Anatolia and got himself elected president of a new Nationalist government, reached a private understanding of their own. The Soviets were given a free hand to overthrow the independent Transcaucasian republics. The Turks were given a free hand to regain Turkish Armenia. In addition, Kemal's Nationalist Army was provided by the Bolsheviks with much-needed weapons and funds to help in removing the European powers—especially the Greeks—from Turkey. By the fall of 1920, the Turks had moved north across the Armenian plateau to a frontier that included Ararat—the border that exists today. The Red Army then entered Erevan and, using the Turkish threat as a lever, "sovietized" the two-year-old Armenian Republic. In March of 1921, the Treaty of Moscow was signed by the Soviet Union and Turkey, formalizing the arrangement. It was a fait accompli, and was accepted by the European powers. In 1922, as a kind of coda to Europe's involvement with the "Armenian Question," Kemal's freshly armed troops pushed the Greek occupying army to the sea at Smyrna, which was set on fire, and there approximately a hundred thousand Greeks and Armenians were killed while Allied warships sat in the harbor.

I thought, In some ways, this has been the most miserable of stories. It made one weep for the hopes of the Armenians: those Armenians who for so many years had trafficked with the liberal sentiments of the West, attending like children to the "interestedness" of certain politicians and missionaries, watching the great nineteenth-century wave of nationalism confer nationhood on states and provinces whose own ethnic "unity" had long been fragmented. For Armenians what else had it been but an illusion, a political dream whose bridge to waking life was mainly this—the inconsistent support of the powerful constitutional democracies of Europe and America? On the other hand, what folly it had been to expect anything else of the world than what had happened! What a persistence of dreaming! Or perhaps in the end it had been a matter neither of folly nor of, let us say, victimization, for there was something quite grandly human in the Armenian experience, with its misfortunes, and pride, and survivorship, and hope: the hope of something better to come, periodically dashed. If the Armenians had been lately afflicted with self-hatred, they had also throughout their existence (like certain children) been afflicted with hopefulness. In some ways, this was probably an affliction like any other, not easily cured.

Far down, below the scattered clouds, there were endless green mountains and, in the distance, a lake and plumes of smoke. Then clouds obscured the ground.

THE PLANE whistled through the hazy air. I slept a long time, or so I thought. At one point, my wife said to me, "Didn't it seem wrong leaving Sarkis behind there?"

"It's his home," I said.

"I know," she said.

"They have hydroelectric stations and computer factories and oranges," I said. "Politics always change."

"I think I know that, too," she said.

ANOTHER TIME—perhaps it was only moments after the first question, or maybe it was an hour later—my wife said, "Do you know why I wished they hadn't kept those two books?"

"They cost money."

"No. In the Svetlana book there was the craziest reference to your father. I was going to show you."

The air in the cabin was warm and heavy. It all felt like part of a dream: I was half waking, half asleep.

"I didn't know they knew each other," I said. "What was it?"

"It was about your father's book *The Green Hat*. Her mother read it shortly before she committed suicide, and Stalin claimed that it had brought about her death. Had you heard that?"

No, I hadn't. I thought, How queer everything is sometimes—how unutterably *queer*. It was probably true—Stalin supposing his wife to have been corrupted by a modish, English, nineteen-twenties novel. My father's novel. A picture came into my mind of Arak trudging through the snow toward old Melikian's house. Armenia at the dawn of the Jazz Age. I thought of Sarkis standing in front of the airport building waving his hand.

"Do you think your father knew about the Stalin story?" my wife asked.

"No, I don't think so," I said.

FOR SOME REASON, I remembered the old women in the market shed, and the piles of radishes. I thought of a certain phrase in Mandelstam's *Journey to Armenia*—a reference to the Armenians' "inexplicable aversion to anything metaphysical." The full quotation runs: "The Armenians' fullness with life, their rude tenderness, their noble inclination for hard work, their inexplicable aversion to anything metaphysical, and their splendid intimacy with the world of real things—all of this said to me, You're awake, don't be afraid of your own time, don't be sly."

Down below, the clouds parted. There was sea—the bright blue of the Mediterranean. We were coming in to land.

We stayed a few days in Istanbul—new Constantinople. Each morning, the sun came up glowing across the Bosporus, which lay a half mile or so below our window: a river of black water filled with little craft, and dozens of ferryboats that crossed incessantly from bank to bank, and sometimes the massive, quiet shape of a Russian tanker returning empty to the Black Sea.

Across the Bosporus stretched the shore of Asia, house-crowded and tree-lined. About two miles upriver, a great new bridge now connected the two sides; it was a graceful green construction, with two tall towers and curving suspension cables. There was talk in the hotel of traffic problems during the rush hour. A little way downriver, right at the edge of the water, stood the gray stone expanse of the Dolmabagdshe Palace, that ponderous, frilly, nineteenth-century strudel of a royal edifice which had been built for the Ottoman sultans by the Armenian architect Balian. "The Armenian architect Balian." It said so right in our Turkish guidebook. And if that was not exactly the only reference to Armenia or Armenians visible in standard Turkish touristic publications, it was nearly so. With the exception of an occasional inclusion in a list of the "polyglot mixture of ancient races" that had once inhabited "pre-

Turkic Asia Minor," the name, the presence, the idea of Armenians appeared to no longer exist in modern Istanbul. It was not so much that there was no sense of an Armenia here (in this nation that contained the classic home of the Armenians), for in political terms that was comprehensible; it reflected a political fact. What seemed less comprehensible and much harder to accept was the extent to which the Armenian connection had been erased. The slate had been wiped bare, as though by an act of will—or, if not absolutely bare, then as close to absolutely bare as was possible.

The first afternoon, I remember, we drove past an old church, so unmistakably Armenian, with its conical roof, that we asked our Turkish guide if we might stop. "It's a Greek church," he said. "I know it very well. It is of no interest."

My wife said, "It looks Armenian."

"There is nothing Armenian around here," the guide said. "It is Greek." And he drove on.

Later, we went back on our own. On the ancient stone above the church entrance, part of the Armenian lettering had been literally erased—rubbed off. But not all of it. The church itself was closed, and a new apartment house had been built in such a way as to wall off the side entrance and the stained-glass windows. Two men in rough clothes were playing cards at a table in the alley. One of them looked at us quizzically.

"Armenian church?" my wife asked.

One of the men shook his head and said something in Turkish. The other man scowled and got to his feet. We left the alley.

"I didn't like that," my wife said as we walked down a more crowded street.

"He didn't understand us," I said.

I don't think that either of us thought he hadn't understood us.

Once, I knew, Istanbul had been filled with Armenian churches and with Armenians. Armenians had formed a key element in the life of the great city—especially, perhaps, as artisans and craftsmen. I had read how in the late Byzantine period, when the western arch of Justinian's Saint Sophia collapsed, an Armenian architect had been called in to study the problems of stress and geometry, and undertake the restoration. Later, when Muhammad the Conqueror captured Constantinople, the people he summoned to build up his new capital were the Armenians and the Greeks, and also the Arabs.

For centuries (regardless of their political position), Armenian artisans had been masters of tilework, of stone-cutting, masters at working with things—perhaps that anti-metaphysical instinct that Mandelstam had spoken of. How strange, then, to be in Istanbul and learn that it had never happened. "Observe this unusual tilework," another guide remarked, pointing to some beautiful orange and blue tiles that adorned a sixteenth-century mosque.

"Who made the tiles?" a fellow tourist asked.

"Turkish craftsmen," said the guide. "There were some Arab tilemakers, too."

On the outside of the mosque stood several twenty-foot columns of basalt, each elaborately, even obsessively, adorned with stone-cut designs that were the familiar geometric figures we had observed on so many old Armenian churches—even the smooth, eroded shapes of grapes and pomegranates I remembered from the fallen cornices at Garni and Zvartnots.

"Who did the stonework?" I asked.

The Turkish guide was middle-aged and accommodating. He gazed upward, examining the designs, which he had surely looked upon each day. "Turkish stonecutters from Anatolia," he replied.

In a sense, all this felt unreal, and almost comical. I realized that I had traveled a long distance from my previous disdain of most things Armenian to my present barely suppressed chauvinism in Istanbul. Perhaps too far. (Had I really become offended by that remark about Anatolian stonecutters?) On the other hand, I felt something faintly evil in the air. Or perhaps it was this: As an Armenian, for the first time I had a sniff, a scent, of what it was like to be hated for being Armenian. Because what was it except hatred to say that a people did not exist?

ONE MORNING, we went to visit another Armenian church. There were a few Armenian churches listed in the phone book. We picked one out, wrote down the address, and asked a driver to take us there. He seemed surprised and then amused that we should want to go to such a place. "Much better Greek church near the hotel," he said. He was a young man with a friendly manner and explained that he wished to save us trouble.

We went anyway, and on our arrival I could appreciate the driver's preference for the Greek church. We were in a shabby part of town, a place of narrow, dirt-strewn streets and few people. The Armenian church seemed run-down and derelict: cracked walls, no paint, few ornaments of any kind. Although it was evidently still in use, it seemed like an abandoned shell; there was something of the look of a cave about it. Next door, however, there was an Armenian school, its courtyard swarming with children. I had grown accustomed in Erevan to seeing large numbers of Armenians, and these Armenian faces in Istanbul seemed surprisingly familiar. Indeed, these children were like children everywhere—energetic, shy, curious. In broken French and English, they asked about the Beatles and Bob Dylan. We replied in kind. Then an Armenian priest appeared. I told him we were Armenians from America. He seemed vague and unresponsive, and led us away from the children into a tiny office, where he sat down behind a small, bare desk and, from its lower drawer, produced an electric hot plate and a jar of instant coffee and a saucepan, which he proceeded in silence to assemble into three cups of coffee.

The coffee made and sipped, I tried to ask him routine

questions about the school. The priest's English was not bad, but his desire for conversation seemed slight. Talking with him was like interviewing a government official on a sensitive subject. I wondered what the sensitive subject was. On his desk was a small plastic Turkish flag, and behind the flag were two photographs—one of Mustafa Kemal, the other of the present Turkish president. What I had wanted to ask him, or somebody, was: What was it like to be an Armenian in Turkey now? Was it hard? Was it easy? Was it routine? My wife pointed to the flag on his desk and asked him if he felt more Turkish or more Armenian. The priest had been talking in a slow monotone about the school curriculum, and changed neither the rhythm nor the subject of his discourse. When he finished, he sipped his coffee.

I finally asked him, "Well, how is it being an Armenian in Turkey today?"

The priest looked pained, or else confused. He gave a sort of smile, and a sort of shrug. He replied something in such a low voice that I couldn't hear it and asked him again.

He looked across at me. "I am sorry, but I have the answers only to other questions," he said.

After leaving the Armenian priest, with his Turkish *drapeau de la patrie* and his photograph of Kemal, I felt depressed, although I knew that this was a foolish response. After all, I lived in America and was American. He lived in Turkey and was Turkish. All the same, there were some differences. Earlier, I had wondered how even in Abdul-Hamid's time Armenians could have chosen to continue living in Turkey. And what in hell's name was any Armenian doing here now? I thought of Erevan, with its inelegance and dust, its rocks and factory smoke and pink stone apartment buildings, its Stalinist graves, its airport police, its decided lack of anything as lovely as the Bosporus at sunset, and thought, Well, at least you were on some kind of solid ground there—you were somebody there.

BACK IN OUR HOTEL, we had arranged to have drinks with some American acquaintances: friends of a New York friend—two professors of English who had taught for many years at the American college up the Bosporus. It was a pleasant, even romantic time in the late afternoon, the garden smelling sweetly in the still air, the coolness of the shade settling around us. It was easy to imagine at such a moment why Constantine had chosen to place his new Rome here, why the failing Byzantines had stayed on and on and on, why Sultan Muhammad had taken care not to destroy too much on his arrival.

We chatted of this and that. The expatriate professors seemed politely interested in our travels but obviously perplexed as to why even an Armenian should wish to sojourn in Soviet Armenia. It was a bit like trying to explain living in Chicago to a Bostonian. "Of course, the Armenians were once a sizable population in Istanbul," said one of the professors, a man in his fifties—thin, sparely elegant, tweedy, perhaps himself a Bostonian.

"There doesn't seem to be much sign of them here any more," I said.

"Yes, it's a pity," he said. "But you must understand the Turkish point of view. The Armenians were a great nuisance to the Turks, and, after all, the country belonged to them. Those things are probably brutal, but they're life."

"They were a nuisance? How?" my wife asked sharply.

The professor smiled. "Well, I'd have imagined you'd know that by now. It's surely in books. I mean that the truth which seems to emerge from those dreadful massacres is that the Armenians basically provoked them, you know— more than anyone would admit to at the time."

"That's true," said the other professor—a younger man, with glasses and a seersucker jacket. "I have several Armenian friends here, and they all readily agree to that. They say, 'On account of the crimes of selfish revolutionaries, we were nearly wiped out.' Actually, you know, even the massacres weren't quite as terrible as they were made out to be."

We all had a fight—one of those dispirited, civilized fights in which the other side is terribly cool and conversational and doesn't care very much. "My dear fellow, as I'm sure you know," the older professor kept intoning, ever calmer and more controlled. Our side verged on shrillness and disarray. I heatedly quoted statistics, doubtless with the air of someone making them up on the spot. "Yes, that's very interesting," said the other professor, gazing out toward the water. Finally, my wife said, "I think you're both fools for sitting here on your damned Bosporus and not knowing what really happened." It was one of those scenes that cause people at other tables to begin to turn their heads and the waiters to become unusually attentive. The two American professors (our new friends) became ever more cultivated and ironic. "Damned Bosporus?" said the older man slowly and quizzically, as if the point at issue were now an attack on an innocent body of water. "My dear, I'm not sure I really care to argue on that level." Well, no. In the end, nothing of further interest was said; no views were exchanged. We somehow patched the "disagreement" together on the surface, and ordered the additional, unwanted drinks in order to show that we were all chums, and gulped them down, and said goodbye. "Be certain to say hello to Henry back in New York!" the tweedy professor called, disappearing into the twilight. Yes, we'll be certain to, we said. Civilization triumphs.

Upstairs in our room, my wife said, "No wonder so many Armenians sound so shrill."

"You mean, because 'nothing happened'?"

"Because the Turks don't admit to anything. And nobody else still gives a damn. There's no release."

It never seemed more true than there in Istanbul. The Armenians were once a great nuisance. The sounds of a dance band floated up to us from the hotel gardens. The lights along the Asia Minor coast began to glow—yellow reflections in the dark Bosporus, where two large cruise ships had lately moored, their masts lit up like Christmas trees. The sky above and around us was a dark blue, grow-

ing darker: still and deep and almost transparent. The bell
of a ferryboat clanged far away. I thought of what I had
seen and read about, trying to hold on to at least the texture
of what it was. Actually, you know, even the massacres
weren't quite as terrible as they were made out to be.

Yellow flowers burning in a metal bowl. The music of a
South American song throbbed lightly against the windowpanes—a girl's voice and guitars.

THE NEXT DAY, I couldn't stand the thought of touring
any more Turkish mosques. The younger of the two professors had telephoned in the morning with a suggestion
that we might wish to be introduced to a friend of his—a
Mr. Dermejian, an elderly Armenian, although brought up
by Turkish foster parents, educated at Oxford, a gentleman
of many cultural interests, most charming, a connoisseur of
Iranian art. Somehow, I could not abide, either, the thought
of meeting Mr. Dermejian, for all his cultural interests and
charm. I imagined that he, too, wore English tweeds, or else
a Magdalen College boating blazer. I could see his pale, soft
hands resting on an old Iranian chessboard. My dear fellow,
you must understand, the affair was blown quite out of
proportion.

Instead, without having any conscious plan in mind, I
walked over to the Istanbul phone directory and began flip-
ping through the pages to the letter "K." Kouyoumjian: my
father's family name. Indeed, there were four or five Kou-

youmjians listed, and that didn't surprise me, for it was a common Armenian name and it was evident that there were still a fair number of Armenians living in Istanbul. There was even a Dikran Kouyoumjian—my father's exact name. On impulse, I picked up the phone and asked the operator for the number.

Against my ear I could hear the other phone ringing, ringing. Then a click. A man's voice answering in Turkish.

"Hello," I said, wondering if I should hang up, wondering what would happen next.

The man's voice changed. "Hello," he said with an educated but imperfect English inflection.

I explained that I was an Armenian from America. That my father's name had been Dikran Kouyoumjian. That although we surely weren't related in any way, I had seen his name in the phone directory and had called to say hello.

"But you must come over," he said.

We talked briefly of the Kouyoumjian family. "There was a distant branch in Bulgaria, then England," he said. "Perhaps your father was connected to that one."

I said, "Yes."

"You and your wife must come for tea," he said.

In the hot midafternoon, we drove down one of the main boulevards, crowded with traffic, then through a network of narrow side streets, also crowded, into another shabby section of town. Our driver—the same sweet young Turk who had taken us to the Armenian church and elsewhere—let us off on a narrow, unkempt street lined for the most part with small, dark shops; it had scattered newspapers and orange peelings on the pavement, and all manner of filth in the gutters. At the end of the street there was a modest four-story apartment house of crumbling brown stucco. Some urchins played inside the lobby, or what had once been a lobby. Kouyoumjian was on the fourth floor.

He opened the door—a pleasant, quiet, slightly smiling man of perhaps fifty. His hair was thinning to the point of baldness, but otherwise he seemed in good trim. In fact, he had the appearance of a fairly successful professional man, or else a small-shop owner. He was an engineer, he said—an electrical engineer. His apartment, sheltered from the grubbiness of the street, seemed composed and well furnished. There were chests and tables, rather massive but highly polished. A bowl of cut flowers stood on a mantelpiece. There were some pinkish crystal glasses in a glass case which made me think for a second of Sarkis's house outside Erevan, with its Czech glassware and well-polished furniture.

On the table in the main room there was an array of English books: *Lord Jim, The Mayor of Casterbridge, Pride and Prejudice,* a thick Oxford dictionary.

I said, "Are you studying literature?"

"I am trying to learn English in order to emigrate to Australia," Kouyoumjian said. "I have been studying for three years." He looked at us shyly, as if we might not understand, or approve.

I thought, Everything becomes clearer. An Armenian

still in Turkey—my father's namesake, even. Dikran Kouyoumjian, of Istanbul, with the orange-leavings and mosques and recorded-prayer minarets of this finally Muslim city outside his windows, and, inside, the domestic talismans of the Armenians: the clean, polished furniture, the cut flowers, the careful displays of glassware. And now, at last, the escape route: Joseph Conrad, Thomas Hardy, and Jane Austen. Australia.

"Are you sorry to be leaving?" I asked.

"It is no good here any more," Kouyoumjian said. "I think it has probably not been good here for Armenians for a long while, but it is difficult to know these things when it is your home." Then, "But I love Istanbul." It seemed such a heartfelt statement, almost as if he were saying it to himself. "My father always loved Istanbul," he went on. "It was he who brought us back here, after the war. I think that was a mistake, for we had been living in Paris, but he said he loved this city. He loved to drive down toward the coast in the spring and see the orchards and flowers." Then, "I think he thought it would get better here after the war."

Kouyoumjian smiled. He seemed not to be a tough man. One imagined that the tough Armenians in Turkey had been killed long ago, or else had extricated themselves. No, he was a modest man, but in a difficult position; he was trying for something difficult. "Sometimes I become afraid when I think of leaving. You see, I am fifty-one years old and have a nice business here. Also, the Turks will let me take no money with me. It is a fact that they want all the

Armenians to leave Turkey. They want no trace of Armenians in Turkey any more—and most of the Armenians have already gone. I think there are only about fifteen thousand remaining. But they will not let us take anything with us. They will not even let us take what we can get for selling our possessions. In Australia, I must start again with nothing."

"What finally made you want to leave?" I asked.

"Because it finally made my heart sick," he said. "You know, under the old sultans they called us 'giaour' and kept us down. Today, they still do the same thing. 'Father, what is "giaour"?' my daughter said when she first went off to school. 'Are we "giaour"?' It is true—for a while I thought things became better. But I was deluding myself. Lately, there has been a growth of Muslim feeling here—especially in the countryside, which is where it usually starts. A while ago, do you remember, there was an incident in America: a crazy old Armenian in California shot two Turks in a hotel. There was a trial about it over there. But here Turkish mobs took to the streets. You could see that they had been officially encouraged. In Erzurum, they hanged two Armenians as reprisal, and beat many others. In Istanbul, they were prepared to hang perhaps a dozen, but they thought it might be noticed, and so instead they beat them savagely, and one of the Armenians can no longer see. I think I finally despaired of life getting better here for our children."

Kouyoumjian's wife entered the room, carrying a tray of tea and little European cakes. She was a quite tall and handsome woman, fair-haired, with her hair piled up—seemingly European. In fact, she was French, and spoke English haltingly. "I worry, too, how we will do in Australia," she said. "But I hear they are kind there. I am glad that Dikran reads all these books. He says, 'I may not speak much English, but I speak fine English.'"

"How has it been, living all these years side by side with the Turks?" I asked.

"There has been no trouble," said Kouyoumjian.

"We have many Turkish friends," said his wife, as if it would be disloyal to suggest otherwise.

"The Turks are nice people, gentle people," said Kouyoumjian. "But sometimes they have a craziness. A crazy feeling comes over them."

"Is it only crazy?" I asked. "It isn't that they hate Armenians?"

Kouyoumjian looked into his teacup, then over at his wife. "I suppose there is some truth in that," he said.

In some ways, it was a charming and hospitable moment—the four of us seated in that small, carefully tended apartment, sipping tea and eating cakes, while Dikran Kouyoumjian discoursed on the good and bad points of life for an Armenian among the Turks. But it was also a bit eerie, as if something were being left out—not so much unsaid as unthought, beyond thought. One knew that a curse had been placed on the Armenians in Turkey, and here we were—in Turkey, smelling the curse. It hovered over Kouyoumjian's cut flowers and plate of little cakes. It waited on the outskirts of our conversation. But no one would name it. Perhaps it was unnamable.

My wife asked if they had other children. It turned out that they had a son about twenty-two years old, who had already gone to Australia. One could see that Kouyoumjian was very proud of his son. "He trained here as an engineer also," he said. "He did very well in the national examinations here, and on the strength of his final score he was given a good job in an important company. But then the man looked at his name—clearly an Armenian name. The man said that he was sorry but he had made a mistake—the position was already taken. This happened once again—in fact, I think more than once—and then my son decided to go to Australia. He has a job in an engineering firm in Sydney."

So that was it, I thought. The young were at last going to extricate the Armenians. I looked at our host and his shy French wife—Dikran Kouyoumjian, with his pleasant face and polite, uncertain manner, his engineer's skill, his volumes of Conrad and Jane Austen on the tabletop, his pink crystal glasses, and bald head, and many friends among the Turks—and thought, How could you have come back from France when they didn't want you here, when they so didn't want you? And then I thought, I bet that your son is tall and impatient, and that you can't tell him anything.

I had one more question, which I wanted to phrase courteously, with due respect. In the end, I simply said, "But why did it take you so long to leave?"

Kouyoumjian looked at me as if he were uncertain what I meant. Then he reached over and touched my arm in the Armenian manner, and leaned back in his chair. "I could give many reasons for why I stayed so long—my business here, our children in school, perhaps the hopes we had right after the war. I have thought about such things often since my son left, for now I have to follow him. A middle-aged man following his son. I think the reason I stayed so long was this—that it was home."

Kouyoumjian's wife stood up and moved behind her husband, her hands on his shoulders. "I've never known any people to care so much about their *homes* as the Armenians," she said, as if neither approving it nor disapproving it. A fact of life.

"But soon we are going away," said Kouyoumjian. And just then he seemed not at all uncertain, not regretful, or even modest: a decent man, a decent middle-aged man following his impatient son; perhaps even shortly to be released from something—an unnamable curse.

At the door, Kouyoumjian extended his hand and shook mine with sudden firmness. "Someday, I hope I will travel to America," he said. "I hear Armenians are happy there."

"As happy as anyone else," I said.

Then he said, "If you have a chance, you should drive down toward our coast. Not on the coast but before the coast there are such flowers, such fruit! Truly, there is a sweetness there. We try to make a motor trip each spring." He waved goodbye.

And so we left. Kouyoumjian in his shirtsleeves, hand outstretched. Kouyoumjian sailing close to the edge of the earth. Behind him, the teacups and half-eaten cakes and *Pride and Prejudice* on the table. We left crowded, shambly, half-elegant Istanbul—the One Great City—with its Bosporus, and curving mosques, and jostle of shipping; the blue-black Bosporus, with its banks of trees, and great green bridge, and tankers gliding by in the twilight.

We never went south toward the flowers and fruit.

Back in New York, some time later, my wife said one evening, "Then does the Armenian story end with Kouyoumjian going to Australia? With Sarkis in Erevan, waving behind the police? Here in America?"

It seemed to me that probably the only point to the "Armenian story" was that it continued. As with other aspects of nature—a waterfall, a rock—there was no way to gauge the merit or demerit of its existence, but the persistence was worth noting. Ultimately, there was bound to be a kind of nobility in this persistence.

BACK IN AMERICA. An Armenian American traveler returned from a voyage among the Armenians—in some ways like the proverbial Indian who has been brought up by white men and who years later makes and returns from a visit to his old tribe. *Where do you stand now, sir? Are you with us or with them?* Alas, by then the alternatives are mostly rhetorical.

The texture of my life is American. My kin are the Armenians. Sometimes like brothers, other times like cousins—even distant cousins. At times, I wish we were closer, but it is not always a sincere wish. We are as close as we will be.

I often wonder what it really is to be *Armenian* in our world—what message it is that we Armenians carry down from our own journey through the centuries. One hears of "Armenian culture"—at least, from Armenians—but it is surely not that. Or the smoky gravity of the Armenian Church. Or even mercantilism—the "trading instinct." For Armenians have turned out to have no greater racial bent for commerce than most other educated peoples—certainly not since the Western nations discarded the pretense of dressing up their shopkeepers as hearty yeomen (nature's noblemen) and joined the group.

Armenians were a—one cannot quite call them a "nation," but at any rate they were a presence long before the world conceived of nations and nationhood in the modern fashion. They are a presence even now—scattered about the globe, or gathered once again, as in tiny Soviet Armenia, in the province of yet another ambitious empire. Armenians, or some of them, at times profess a passion for this nationhood—this organism like the ones from whose madness and pride the Armenians have suffered as much as any people. But perhaps in the end the message of the Armenians is more particular than mere persistence. Perhaps, if there exists a deeper possibility in the psyche of this ancient, sturdy, and minor race, it is this: the capacity of a people for proceeding *beyond* nationhood. For to be a nation—a member of a modern nation—is to inherit territory, and pride in property, and to be connected to collective dreams of quite impossible grandeur and savagery, fertility and hatred. To be an Armenian has meant that one has been compelled by circumstance to rise above or fall below—or, anyway, to skirt—these so-called imperatives of nationhood and property, and thus has been free to attempt the struggle of an ordinary life, and to dream more modest dreams, and to try to deal with one's dreams as best one could. Oh, it is true that for some years Armenian dreams were in a most dreadful tangle. The kings of Nairi enmeshed in liberal political adventures. The kings of Nairi dreaming dreams of grandeur, adrift in foreign courts. Mountain kings with crowns of branches and palaces of rock. Such unmetaphysical kings! But this much seems to be also true: there is a good chance now that the clearheaded, impatient young will begin to set their fathers free.

I HAVE THOUGHT OFTEN about my father since our journey, although I no longer dream about him as much. Once, I remembered a dream of his that he had told me long ago—I think the only dream I ever heard him describe. And then it was with rather gruff perplexity, for it was during the last year of his life, when he slept unevenly—frequently sleeptalking, or waking in starts. It had been about *his* father. "You know, he was just as I remembered him as a boy," my father said that morning. "Except his hair was white—but very thick. He wore a frock coat and steel-rimmed spectacles. He stood at the end of our road speaking to me, calling. But he was speaking in Armenian, and I couldn't understand a word."

Sometimes I think it is as if a circle, once broken, had been completed or recompleted. What circle? We were kin to begin with.

Notes

- Quote by Saroyan, pg. 51 → 'Armenia is there'

- Pg. 78, chauvinism of misfortune

- pg. 92, discussion of WWII, & Armenians as having no use for war, in light of the conflict in Nagorno-Karabakh

- geographic distinction between upper + lower Armenia. pg. 96

- City of Sis, pg. 98

- The aspiration of an entire people? pg. 169

- "The Turkish massacres & "deportations" of the Armenians were the most notable early example of the employment of modern communications + technology in the acting out + realization of political violence". pg. 243

- The French wife on Armenians attached to home, pg. 288

- "A Return to Nationhood?" → post-Soviet Armenia, pg. 291-292